ıME AUTHOR

ndian Nationalism

Contemporary India

and Politics in Modern India

nalism in Modern India

;e and Growth of Economic Nationalism

Indian Natio

The Long-Ter

BY THE S

Essays on

Essays on

Ideology

Commu

The Ri

Indian National Movement

The Long-Term Dynamics

Bipan Chandra

HAR-ANAND
PUBLICATIONS PVT LTD

Published by Ashok Gosain and Ashish Gosain for:
HAR-ANAND PUBLICATIONS PVT LTD
E-49/3, Okhla Industrial Area, Phase-II, New Delhi-110020
Tel: 41603490
E-mail: info@haranandbooks.com/haranand@rediffmail.com
Shop online at: www.haranandbooks.com

Reprint, 2025

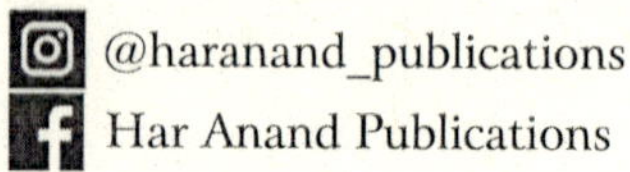

Printed in India

To
G.M. Telang and Mohit Sen,
old friends by whom
I have been encouraged

Preface

This work, presented in an earlier version as Presidential Address to the Indian History Congress in 1985, represents the findings of collective research in India's national liberation struggle in which I have been engaged along with my colleagues Mridula Mukherjee, Aditya Mukherjee and Sucheta Mahajan.

In particular, the emphasis is on setting forth a framework for understanding the strategic discussion of the freedom struggle, especially during the period of Gandhi's leadership. Different phases of the struggle and its different forms—extra-legal mass movements on a scale unsurpassed in world history, constitutional activity, constructive work and day-to-day political-ideological propaganda and agitation through the Press, platform, literature and songs—are sought to be analyzed within this strategic framework.

There is also a discussion of certain other crucial aspects of the movement such as its ideological and programmatic dimensions, the role and significance of non-violence, the relationship between the leaders and the masses, its ideological and organizational open-endedness and the potentiality of its ideological transformation.

In addition to archival work, private papers, collected and selected works of Mahatma Gandhi, Jawaharlal Nehru, Rajendra Prasad and other leaders, these findings are based on our interviews all over the country with over 1,500 persons who took active part in the freedom struggle from the village to the *taluka*, provincial and all-India levels or who worked as part of the colonial administrative apparatus, and we gratefully acknowledge their co-operation and hospitality.

Many friends and students, apart from my co-workers, have contributed to the making of this study. In particular, I am thankful to Sashi Joshi, Bhagwan Josh, K.K.N. Kurup, V. Ramakrishna and Lalitha Ramakrishna, C.S. Krishna and Usha Krishna, Shantha Sinha, G. Rudrayya Chowdari, K. Gopalan Kutti, J.P. Rao, Keshavan Veluthat, Gangadrharan Nambiar, A. Murali, Mohan Das, Rajendra Prasad, Narendra Panjwani, Miriam Dossal, Medha and Vijay Lele, Visalakshi Menon, Anthony Thomas and Gyanesh Kudaisya for helping us conduct interviews as well as providing us stimulus through discussion. I would also like to acknowledge a special debt to the late Arutha Ramachandra Reddy, a veteran of the Telengana struggle, who took us around the Telengana villages at the advanced age of 75. Our ideas have been formed over the years through intense discussions with S. Gopal, Romila Thapar, Mohit Sen, K.N. Panikkar, S. Bhattacharya, Kewal Varma, P.C. Joshi, Ravindar Kumar, V.N. Datta, Barun De, A.R. Desai, Lajpat Jagga, D.N. Gupta, Bikash Chandra, Sanjay Prasad, Sangeeta Singh and Ravi Vasudevan.

I am very thankful to the Directors of National Archives and of State archives at Madras, Hyderabad, Trivandrum, Bombay, Lucknow and Patna and the library staff of the JNU for extending their facilities. Of course, no research on the Indian national movement is today possible without the cooperation of the Director and staff of the Nehru Memorial Museum and Library which has been extended to me and my co-workers in full measure. I am also very grateful to the Indian Council of Social Science Research without whose financial assistance the larger project of which this short study is a part would not have been possible. I am also thankful to Prof. M.S. Agwani, the then Vice-Chancellor of J.N.U., and Prof. Irfan Habib, the then Chairman of the Indian Council of Historical Research, for funding the transcription of some of the interviews from cassets.

As in the case of my previous work, Usha, my wife, has participated actively in the making of the present one.

BIPAN CHANDRA

Contents

CHAPTER 1

Introduction and Preview

Before I take up its long-term dynamics, we have to decide what was the Indian National Congress (INC). In my view, the Congress was the leader of the popular anti-imperialist movement of the Indian people; and its activities in the main constituted this movement.[1] The task of politicizing, activizing and mobilizing the Indian people was accepted by the Congress from beginning but was basically undertaken after 1918. In the Gandhian era, the national movement derived its entire force from the militancy and self-sacrificing spirit of the masses. Starting out as the activity of the radical nationalist intelligentsia, the national movement later succeeded in mobilizing the youth, the women, the urban petty bourgeoisie, the urban and rural poor, the urban and rural artisans, and large sections of the peasantry and small landlords.

Despite its many weaknesses, the Congress became, and remained until independence, the symbol—as well as the chief vehicle and organizer and the representative—of the anti-imperialist or national liberation struggle. The movement led by the Congress was, with all its positive and negative factures, the actual, historically existing anti-imperialist movement of the Indian people.[2] It was in this

[1]We must distinguish the pre-1947 Congress from the post-1947 Congress. After 1947, it gradually became a regular political party with a different character, class content, leadership pattern, etc.

[2]This aspect was well summed up in the preamble to the resolution on the national demand moved by Jayaprakash Narayan at the Tripuri session of the Congress in March 1930: "The Congress has, for more than half a century, striven for advancement of the people of India and it has represented the urge of the Indian people towards freedom and self-expression. During the past twenty years, it has engaged itself, on behalf of the masses

movement that the historical energies and genius of the Indian people were incorporated, as is the case with any genuine mass movement.

This point needs to be stressed because in recent years the neo-colonial school of historians, continuing the tradition of the spokespersons and ideologues of the colonial regime, which flourished from 1880 onwards, have shown almost a missionary zeal in denying the legitimacy of the national movement. They also do so either by denying its anti-imperialist character or by holding up against it actual or potential or 'parallel' anti-imperialist streams declaring the actual movement to be 'a fraud suppressing the real urges of the Indian people.' They find it impossible to accept that the Indian people and their leaders, via the Congress-led national movement, were as much engaged in fighting a national war as were the Irish, the Chinese since 1925, the Soviet people during 1917-21 and 1941-45, the British during 1939-45 or the French (resistance) from 1940-45, and were conscious of the fact.[3] Therefore, these historians cannot also accept that the same categories of nation, class, motivation, mobilization, ideology, etc., should be used to analyze the Indian national movement as are used to study these other movements.[4]

There were of course many other strands in India's struggle for freedom: The Revolutionaries from 1897 to 1947, the Akali movement of the early 1920s, the Indian National Army during the World War II, the State Peoples' movements, the various tribal peoples' struggles, etc. Though many of these remained outside the

of India, in a struggle against British imperialism, and through the suffering, discipline and sacrifice of the people, it has carried the nation a long way to independence, that is, its objective." Quoted in D. G. Tendulkar, *Mahatma*, Vol. 5, p. 65.

[3]See, for example, M. K. Gandhi, *Collected Works* (CW), Vol. 68, pp. 240-1. Gandhi often used the simile of war to describe the character of the political activities of the Congress.

[4]See Bipan Chandra, et. al., *Economic and Political Weekly*, 6 May 1984.

organizational framework of the Indian National Congress, there was no Chinese wall separating them from the Congress. At no stage did they become alternatives to the mainstream of the national movement[5] nor were they ever quantitatively and qualitatively in the same class. It was the Congress-led movement in which millions upon millions of both sexes and all classes, castes, religions and regions to a greater or lesser extent participated. The Congress, being not just a party but a movement, incorporated within itself different political and ideological trends as well.

The study of the INC has therefore to be at the heart or centre of the study of India's anti-imperialist struggle, though it need not occupy the sole position.[6]

That the Indian national movement had developed and then propagated on a large scale an economic and political critique of British colonialism in India is now well-known and its struggle for democracy and civil liberties and secularism is also being increasingly acknowledged.

It is however seldom realized that the leadership of the movement had also gradually, overtime, developed a political strategy for the movement primarily geared to weakening and destroying colonial hegemony over the Indian people.

The existing writings on the subject have failed to deal with, or even discuss, this strategy.[7] It appears as if the movement was a mere conglomeration of different struggles or in the case of the Gandhian phase certain principles such as non-violence and certain forms of struggle such as satyagraha, *picketing*, etc., without an overall strategy.

[5]The only large-scale popular movement which may be said to have formed part of an alternative stream of politics (though not of anti-imperialist) were the communal and casteist movements which were not nationalist and which invariably, sooner or later, betrayed loyalist, pro-colonial tendencies. See my *Communalism in Modern India*, Chapter 4.

[6]Just as is the case with the study of the Bolshevik Party in the Russian Revolution and the role of the Communist Party in the Chinese Revolution.

[7]One exception is Gene Sharp.

The Indian National movement was perhaps the first example in the world of struggle for hegemony which, by definition, is not a one-time struggle for political power but a long-term struggle for influence over the minds of the people and control of state power through such influence, or, in Antonio Gramsci's phrase, not seizure of power through one continuous assault but gradual control over the vast terrain surrounding state power.

The beginnings of this approach were made with Dadabhai Naoroji, the acknowledged leader of the early phase of the nationalist movement. He initiated and developed a critique of the underdevelopment of India by colonialism, thus undermining a basic component of colonial hegemony. As the struggle for India's freedom developed and increasingly acquired a strong base among the intelligentsia and the educated youth, Naoroji pointed out in a letter to D.E. Wacha (General Secretary of the Indian National Congress and its President in 1901) that the political strategy of the movement would have to be based on the nature of the response of the colonial regime to it.[8]

The Swadeshi Movement from 1905 to 1908 and Lokamanya Tilak's and Annie Besant's Home Rule Leagues developed this strategy further during 1915 to 1919. It was, however, Gandhiji who, even when learning from his predecessors, put his distinctive stamp on the movement and gradually developed a distinct strategy of political struggle against colonial rule.

Even while acknowledging the role of his predecessors, the present work is primarily a study of the Gandhian political strategy.

Gandhiji was a multisided personality, who had views on most aspects of life and times. But he was above all a leader and strategist

[8]"The very discontent and impatience it (the Congress) has evoked against itself as slow and non-progressive among the rising generation are among its best results or fruits. It is its own evolution and progress. (the task is) to evolve the required revolution— whether it would be peaceful or violent. The character of the revolution will depend upon the wisdom or unwisdom of the British Government and action of the British people." Quoted in M.R. Masani, *Dadabhai Naoroji, The Grand Old Man of India*, 1939, p. 441.

of a mass movement for political non-violent liberation and he saw himself as such. But his work and vision went beyond mere Indian political struggle. He was, above all, committed to struggle against all forms of oppression, discrimination and domination. He strongly opposed communalism, caste oppression, male chauvinism and cultural domination. At the same time he gave primacy to the struggle against colonialism, because he saw it as, to use Mao Ze Dong's phrase, the primary contradiction of the time. But he always saw this as the first of the many struggles for human liberation which he hoped to wage.

His strategy was not a fully blown scheme from the outset of his political career in South Africa or India. It was developed gradually over time. Gandhiji learnt from experience, constantly experimenting and changing to suit the circumstances and the level the movement had reached.[9] Also social scientists have tended to concentrate on Gandhiji's philosophy of life. But, in fact, his philosophy of life had only a limited impact on the people. It was as a political leader and through his political strategy and tactics of struggle that he moved millions into political action in India.

This aspect of Gandhiji as a strategist of mass struggles was so brilliantly, as if in a flash, perceived by Antonio Gramsci, and caught the imagination and got the acceptance of countless persons and movements the world over; for example by Nelson Mandela in South Africa, Martin Luther King (Junior) in the U.S.A., Les Walesa

[9]As he wrote in 1933: "In my search after Truth I have discarded many ideas and learnt many new things and, therefore, when anybody finds any inconsistency between any two writings of mine, if he has still faith in my sanity, he would do well to choose the latter of the two on the same subject." *Harijan*, 29.4.1933, in *CW*, Vol. 55, p.61. He wrote on the same lines in 1938: "During my student days ... I learnt a saying of Emerson I never forgot, 'Foolish consistency is the hobgoblin of little minds,' said the sage. I cannot be a little mind, for foolish consistency has never been my hobgoblin... my recent writings must be held as cancelling my comparatively remote sayings and doings. Though my body is deteriorating through age, no such law of deterioration, I hope, operates against wisdom which I trust is not only not deteriorating but even growing." *Harijan*, 27.8.1938, in *CW*, Vol. 67, p.284.

in Poland, and countless other leaders of mass struggles the world over. As Nelson Mandela put it: "We knew disciplined cadre-based movements and we knew undisciplined mass movements. But Gandhiji taught us how to wage disciplined mass movements."[10]

The basic elements of the Gandhian strategy can be represented in the formula Struggle-Truce-Struggle' (on a higher plane) or S-T-S'. In this strategy phases of extra-legal mass movements alternate with more 'passive' phases, during which political activity is carried on within the confines of the legal space and the struggle proceeds through stages without losing its anti-imperialist edge or sight of the goal of complete independence at any stage.

In this strategy ideological struggle and popular consciousness and the political activity of the masses play central roles. This strategy bears close resemblance to the strategy of war of position as put forward and elaborated by Antonio Gramsci, the Italian Marxist thinker. In fact, the Indian national movement was perhaps the only historical actualization of Gramsci's strategic vision. Our—mine and my co-workers'—analytical framework incorporates the theoretical advances made by Gramsci and under his influence by Marxists the world over. This framework also owes a lot to the understanding and perspectives of those who participated in the freedom struggle and who had clearly internalized its basic features without necessarily theorizing it. As is made clear in the text, Gandhiji was the fountain- head of the strategy, though previous leaders from Dadabhai Naoroji to Lokamanya Tilak had contributed to its evolution. Unlike Lenin and Mao Ze Dong, his two great contemporary strategists of revolution, Gandhiji was not given to putting forward theoretical formulations. But strewn among his writings and interviews, especially during the years 1933-42, are brilliant strategic formulations which combined with his concrete political activity add up to a coherent whole.

[10]As narrated by Gopal Gandhi, who was earlier Indian High Commissioner in South Africa.

Basic to Gandhian strategy was the arousal of and reliance upon the energy and creativity of the masses and the cadre of the movement. Non-violence was not a mere personal fad or dogma of Gandhiji nor was it dictated by the interests of the propertied classes, a consequence of the 'bourgeois' character of the movement. It was an essential part of the movement whose strategy involved the waging of a hegemonic struggle based on a mass movement which mobilized the people to the widest possible extent.

In the text I have drawn attention to the role that constitutional activity plays in this strategy, especially the capacity of the national movement to utilize the constitutional space without getting co-opted by the colonial state. It did not completely reject this space, as such rejection in democratic or semi-democratic societies entails heavy costs in terms of hegemonic influence and often leads to isolation. It entered and used it effectively in combination with non-constitutional mass struggle to overthrow the existing, colonial structure.

Constructive work – organized around the promotion of khadi, national education, Hindu-Muslim unity, the boycott of foreign cloth and of liquor, the social upliftment of the Harijans ('low' caste 'untouchables') and the tribal people, and the struggle against untouchability—formed an important part of Gandhian strategy, especially during its constitutional or 'passive' phases, in establishing and maintaining contact with the masses and in absorbing the creative energies of the cadre.

Gandhian strategy was based on a complex understanding of the colonial state in India—that it was different from a purely authoritarian or dictatorial state, that it was semi-hegemonic so far as it functioned through the rule of law, a rule-bound bureaucracy and a relatively independent judiciary while simultaneously enacting and enforcing extremely repressive laws, especially during the movement phases of the struggle. It extended a certain amount of civil liberties in normal times and curtailed them in periods of mass struggle. It was based on civil institutions such as local government, an elaborate educational system and a modern Press. It also constantly offered constitutional and economic concessions though it always retained the basics of state power in its own hands. An understanding of the character of society and political forces in Britain also went into the making of this strategy. This was also important because weakening and destroying the opponent's hegemony over his own people and his own instruments of power was an important aspect of Gandhian strategy.

Lastly it is to be noted that all the various elements of Gandhian strategy were not, to Gandhiji, values in themselves or abstract values, but made sense to him only as constituent elements of non-violent struggle for political and social ends. And it is these ends that were to be studied, in the main. As he often advised, resistance to evil was primary and, therefore, if necessary even violent means would be preferred if non-violence could not be practised. And, of course, as he often pointed out, it is not only his words but his work and practice which had to be studied and learnt from.

A few words about the ideological, political dimensions of the Indian National Congress. Being not just a party but a movement, it incorporated within itself different political and ideological trends. As a movement, in its various forms and phases, it took modern politics to the people. It did not, in the main, appeal to their pre-modern consciousness based on religion, caste and locality or loyalty to the traditional rulers or chieftains. It also did not mobilize people ideologically around religion, caste or region. It fought for no benefits on that basis. People did not join it as Brahmins or Patidars or Marathas, or Harijans. Though it made no appeal to caste identities, in some cases caste structure was used in villages to enforce discipline in a movement whose motivation and demands had nothing to do with caste.

Even when relying on popular consciousness, experience, perception of oppression and the needed remedies, on notions of good rule or utopia, the movement did not merely reflect the existing consciousness but also made every effort to radically transform it in the course of the struggle. Consequently, it created space for as well as got integrated with other modern liberationist movements—movements of women, youth, peasants, workers, Harijans and other lower castes.

The national movement based itself from its beginnings in the 1880s on a critique of colonialism and colonialization of the Indian economy, a pro-poor orientation and a basic commitment to political and economic independence, modern economic development, secularism, democracy and civil liberties, and internationalism and independent foreign policy. What is perhaps equally important, it constantly evolved in a left-ward direction under the impact of socialist ideas, individuals and groups. At the same time, as a whole, it remained, despite contending trends, under the hegemony of bourgeois or capitalist developmental perspective. But I have suggested that this was not inevitable. There were many features of the movement and its dominant leadership which created openings for the transformation of the movement towards socialist ideological hegemony. That this did not happen was the result of a complex of forces, including the failure of the left to grasp the character of the Gandhian strategy and ideological framework and to relate to them in a creative and meaningful manner, simulataneously absorbing, developing and transcending them, and thus failing to give the movement a socialist orientation.

In conclusion, it is suggested that the experience of the Indian struggle, or rather national liberation revolution, and especially of its strategic practice, has a particular significance for movements for social transformation and changes in state structure in democratic, semi-democratic or democratic-type hegemonic states and societies. In that sense, it is comparable to the significance of the British, French, Russian, Chinese, Cuban and Vietnamese revolutions.

CHAPTER 2

Ideological and Programmatic Dynamics

The Indian national movement was basically the product of the central or primary contradiction of colonial India, the contradiction between colonialism and the interests of the Indian people. This was its material basis. Its primary long-term dynamic was provided by the fact that it arrived at, and based itself on, a correct grasp of this primary contradiction. On this basis and the basis of its perception of the common interests of the Indian people as also their social experience as a colonized people, it evolved an all-sided understanding of Indian reality and gradually generated, formed and crystallized a clear-cut anti-colonial ideology. It evolved a clear, scientific and firm understanding and analysis of colonialism and the primary contradiction of Indian society and made it visible to the Indian people. Already during the last quarter of the 19th century, the seed-time of Indian nationalism, the founding fathers of the national movement had worked out a clear understanding of the three modes of colonial surplus extraction or exploitation: (a) Directly through taxation, plunder and large-scale employment of Englishmen; (b) unequal trade by making India a hinterland for the production and sale of raw materials and purchase of metropolitan manufactures; (c) investment of British-owned capital. In the drain theory they had evolved a powerful economic instrument for laying bare the overall mechanism of colonial surplus appropriation. They had further grasped that the essence of colonialism lay in the subordination of the Indian economy and society as a whole to the needs of the British economy and society, and that India's colonial relationship was not an accident of history or a result of political policy but sprang rather from the very character of British society and India's subordination to it.[1] This understanding of the complex economic mechanism of modern imperialism was further advanced after 1918 under the impact of the anti-imperialist mass movements and the spread of Marxist ideas. The nationalist leadership also grasped that the central contradiction could be resolved only through the transformation (the Moderate belief) or overthrow of colonial economic relations. Moreover, at each stage of its development, it linked its political analysis to the analysis of colonialism. The anti-colonial world-view was further strengthened by the development of a foreign policy based on anti-colonialsm in other parts of the world.

Our interviews with freedom fighters show that this anti-colonial world-view was fully internalized by the lower-most cadre of the national movement as also by large segments of Indian people.[2]

[1]They were perhaps the first—and certainly before Hobson or Lenin—to evolve a detailed economic critique of colonialism.

[2]That the peasants did indeed understand and appreciate nationalist ideas is clear from the report of the India League Delegation that toured the villages in 1932. Refuting the Simon Commission's understanding that the masses in India were attracted not by "abstract political ideas" but by the personalities of leaders like Gandhi, the India League Delegation noted: "The awakening in the villages is no doubt to a great extent due to personalities like Gandhi, Abdul Ghaffar Khan, Vallabhbhai Patel, Purshottamdas Tandon, Jawaharlal Nehru, Kelapan, and others. But these men have made their appeal on the basis of ideas and facts.... We tested for ourselves in a number of places the extent to which the villager has appreciated the issues, and understood the causes.... We found that the economic and social issues were very live ones. We heard about poverty, taxation, foreign exploitation, neglect of education and all the other factors that are at the back of India's resistance. We found out that the villagers knew what the Congress stood for, and also that they had no illusion about the enormity of the task before the country.... We went on to talk about Swaraj and why they wanted it. We suggested in great detail that their conditions would be better if they had more schools, roads and other facilities, if their taxes were lightened and that to win Swaraj was merely a political business. We expected this to go down and to be told that the material improvements we suggested were all that they really wanted. Instead, an old man who was a working agriculturist himself, told us that Swaraj was a matter of self-respect, freedom, and self-power. Also he felt quite sure that without 'self-power' the conditions which we had mentioned would not be obtained." Report of the India League Delegation, reproduced as "Village Repression by British Rulers" in A.R. Desai, *Peasant Struggles in India,* pp. 305-6.

Thus, the primary contradiction provided the material or structural basis of the national movement and its grasping through the anti-colonial ideology its ideological basis. This opened the way to a firm and consistent anti-imperialist movement which could follow highly flexible tactics precisely because of its rootedness in and adherence to the anti-colonial principle. This also partly explains why the Indian national movement did not waver or surrender before imperialism as did the seemingly more militant movements like those of China from 1911 to 1927. It also made it difficult for colonial authorities to co-opt it even when it was following extremely mild politics under the leadership of Dadabhai Naoroji, M. G. Ranade, Pherozeshah Mehta, Surendranath Banerjea and G.K. Gokhale.[3] On the other hand, once the ideological basis of colonial rule was challenged and eroded, the rise of a militant anti-imperialist movement became inevitable and was a mere matter of time.

In this context, the role of ideology as a basic element of the dynamics of any popular movement needs to be emphasized. The Base-Superstructure relationship and the political dynamics in the case of a movement are very different from those in a situation of static politics. The politics of the French Revolution, or the Russian Revolution, or the popular national liberation movements of Asia, Africa and Latin America (say China, India, Vietnam, Mozambique, Guinea-Bissau, Algeria, Cuba or Nicaragua) or the popular, national resistance movements of Yugoslavia, Italy or France or the Warsaw Ghetto or other countries of occupied Europe cannot be understood by applying the same tools as are used to analyze the factional politics of the reign of George the Third, or Tammany Hall, or Mayor Daley's Chicago, Mr. Reagan, Thatcher or present-day Bihar, UP or Tamil Nadu—though it seems to us that the intellectual tools of Pareto, Mosca, and structuralism-functionalism have failed in a basic manner even in these cases.

[3]On the other hand, the colonial authorities could not only easily conciliate and accept the political demands of the Muslim League in 1907 but even accept the class demands and thus quieten the militant peasants involved in the Indigo Revolt, the Pabna Uprising, and the Deccan Agrarian Riots.

What is more important, ideology and ideological preparation are important in any form of popular, mass-based struggle; they are, however, of crucial importance in hegemonic struggle (which is what we hope to show the Indian freedom struggle was), since the material resources play here a lesser role, and are in any case concentrated in the hands of the dominant side; and the people have, in any case, and first of all, to come to know who the enemy is, and what the central contradiction is. Moreover, passive support or opposition or voting for and against are one thing; but active opposition involving immense sacrifice cannot be offered only on the basis of exploitation or a sense or knowledge of exploitation. It requires strong, very strong ideological commitment.

One reason why many scholars today fail to understand the role of ideology as a basic element of the anti-imperialist movements is the fact that in their own societies the area of common national interests has now been shrinking for decades. Consequently, nationalism has often been used in their societies as a mere 'ideology' or false consciousness or a form of 'bamboozlement' of the people—by the ruling classes and their ideologues. But in colonial societies, such common national interests did and do exist—because of and against colonialism or its heritage, because of the primary or central contradiction. Nationalist (or anti-imperialist or national liberationist) ideology is here a prime mover of history, for even the primary contradiction can be resolved and the people mobilized around it only on the basis of nationalist, anti-colonial ideology. For the same reason, one does not take even the first step towards understanding an anti-colonial movement without studying, analyzing and grasping the central contradiction and the nationalist, anti-colonial ideology. The basic weakness of the neo-colonial schools—and the reason they have to be characterised as neo-colonial—lies precisely in the fact that they ignore, if not deny, the central causative roles that the central contradiction and the anti-imperialist ideology play in the rise and development of the national liberation struggle of the colonial people, in this case the Indian people. Inevitably, they fall back on the contention 'that

Indian nationalism is a myth cloaking what is no more than faction, patronage and collaboration.'

II

Along with the anti-colonial world-view, certain other ideological elements provided the programmatic dynamics of the Indian national movement. These constituted the broad socio-economic-political vision of the national leadership. Broadly speaking, this vision was that of bourgeois or capitalist, independent economic development and a secular, republican, democratic, civil libertarian political order, both the economic and political order to be based on principles of social equality. Interestingly, this vision was to remain unquestioned till 1947 (or even this day); all questioning and controversy was to be confined to the capitalist character of the economic order.

The nationalist movement was fully committed to parliamentary democracy and civil liberties.[4] It provided the soil and climate in which these two could dig deep roots. From its foundation the Indian National Congress was organized along democratic lines. From the beginning the nationalists fought every inch of the way against attacks by the colonial authorities on the freedom of Press, speech and association and other civil liberties. One of the brightest spots in the record of the Congress Ministries during 1937-39 was the visible, massive extension of civil liberties. In fact, civil liberties and parliamentary democracy and the associated parliamentary practices were indigenized during the 19th and 20th centuries not so much by the colonial regime as by the national movement and the nationalist intelligentsia. Civil liberties and democracy in their turn opened the way to the deepening of the social base of the national movement as well as to the evolution of a hegemonic strategy of anti-colonial struggle.

[4]Nehru's commitment to civil liberties is well-known. Here is a quotation from Gandhi: "Civil liberty consistent with the observance of non-violence is the first step towards swaraj. It is the breath of political and social life. It is the foundation of freedom. There is no room there for dilution or compromise. It is the water of life. I have never heard of water being diluted." *Collected Works,* Vol. 69, p. 356. For his definition of civil liberty, see *ibid.,* p. 402.

Secularism was from the beginning made a basic constituent of the nationalist ideology and strong emphasis laid on Hindu-Muslim unity. Caste oppression was opposed and after 1920 abolition of untouchability made a basic constituent of the programme and political work of the national movement. The cause of women was taken up actively. 'Highness and lowness' in society was made a target of general attack. The multi-faceted diversity of the Indian people was fully recognized. That India was not yet a developed or structured nation, but a nation-in-the-making, was accepted and made the basis of ideological work and agitation. The contribution of the objective process of the economic and administrative unification of India under colonial rule was clearly seen. In fact, one reason why the Moderates supported continuation of British rule despite their sharp critique of economic colonialism was the desire that this process should not be interrupted. It was also grasped that common subjection to colonial rule provided the material and emotional basis for nation-making and that, since nation was not given as a prior datum to the national movement, one of the functions of the movement was to structure a nation through a common struggle against colonialism, that the political and ideological practices of the movement would play a crucial role in the process of nation-in-the making. Furthermore, it was clearly understood that the objective of unifying the Indian people into a nation was to be realized by taking full account of regional, religious, caste, ethnic and linguistic differences. The cultural aspirations of the different linguistic groups were given full recognition.

The Congress and the national movement were fully committed to the development of India on the basis of modern industry and agriculture. Moreover, they emphasized the objective of independent economic development including independence from foreign capital, the creation of an independent capital goods sector and the foundation of independent science and technology. In the late 1930s, the objective of economic planning was widely and universally accepted. The ideological commitment to these objectives was further strengthened and not weakened during the

Gandhian era, though it may be added that Gandhi's stand on large-scale industry has been grossly distorted. He repeatedly said that he was not opposed to modern large-scale industry so long as it augmented, and lightened the burden of, human labour and not displaced it and was owned by the state and not private capitalists.[5]

The world-outlook of the Congress and the national movement was also a powerful aspect of the dynamics of Indian nationalism. Over the years, the nationalists evolved a policy of opposition to imperialism on a world scale, and of expressing and establishing solidarity with the anti-imperialist movements in other parts of the world. From the 1870s, they made an effort to establish solidarity with, and get the support of, the anti-imperialist sections of British public life and firmly established the notion that the Indians hated imperialism but not the British. (This principle of non-hatred of the colonizing people was to provide a powerful moral underpinning to the national movement and make the members of the ruling apparatuses pay a high price in terms of their own self-image whenever they adopted ferocious measures to suppress the satyagrahas. It also kept Indian nationalism firmly rooted to anti-imperialism without degenerating into 'reverse' racism of any kind.) They also established general links with the progressive anti-colonial and anti-capitalist forces of the world from Hyndman and the Labour Party's left-wing to the International Socialist Congress, the League against Imperialism, the Soviet Union and the Comintern. The Congress took a clear-cut anti-Fascist stand in the 1930s and gave active support to the anti-Fascist struggles of Ethiopia, Spain, Czechoslovakia

[5]For example, at the end of 1938, thirty economists had a discussion with Gandhi on his economic philosophy. "Are you against large-scale production?" they asked. Gandhi replied: "I never said that. This belief is one of the many superstitions about me. Half of my time goes in answering such things. But from scientists I expect better knowledge. Your question is based on loose newspaper reports and the like. What I am against is large-scale production of things villagers can produce without difficulty." "Do you think that cottage industries and big industries can be harmonized?" they asked. "Yes," said Gandhi, "if they are planned so as to help the villages. Key industries, industries which the nation needs, may be centralized.... Supposing the State controlled paper-making and centralized it, I would expect it to protect all the paper that villages can make." *Collected Works*, Vol. 68, pp. 258-9.

and the Jewish people, and the national liberation struggles of the Arabs against British imperialism and the Chinese against Japanese imperialism. In the 1920s they asked Indian soldiers not to join British imperialism in suppressing the Chinese Revolution and in the 1930s repeatedly asked Indians to boycott Japanese goods.

III

Basic to the dynamics of the national movement was the fact that from the beginning it adopted a pro-poor orientation and accepted and propagated a programme of reforms that was quite radical by contemporary standards and was basically oriented towards the people. Compulsory primary education, lowering of taxation on the poor and lower middle classes, reduction of salt tax, land revenue and rent, debt relief and provision of cheap credit to the agriculturists, protection of tenant rights, workers' right to a living wage and a shorter working day, higher wages for low-paid employees in the colonial bureaucracy including the policemen, defence of workers' and peasants' right to organize themselves, protection and promotion of village industries, eradication of the drink evil, improvement in the social position of women, including their right to work and education and to equal political rights, legal and social measures for abolition of untouchability, and reform of the machinery of law and order were some of the major reformist demands taken up by the nationalist movement.

What is equally important, at no stage was the Congress content with its existing character. It went on continuously defining itself further and further in a radical direction in terms of the popular element. Increasingly, freedom was defined in socio-economic terms which went far beyond mere absence of foreign rule. By the late 1930s, the Indian national movement was one of the most radical national liberation movements. Starting with Dadabhai Naoroji, the pro-poor orientation was immensely strengthened with the coming of Gandhi and the growth of a powerful left during the late 1920s and the 1930s. It found full reflection in its resolutions at Karachi, Lucknow and Faizpur sessions and in the

Election Manifestoes of 1936-37 and 1945-46 and a partial reflection in the economic and social reforms of the Congress Ministries. During the 1930s and the 1940s even the Congress right wing was committed to basic changes in political and economic power. Even the anti-class war resolution passed by the Working Committee in 1934 stood on the ground of the Karachi resolution.[6] Important in this respect was the development of Gandhi in a radical direction. His life work was, of course, always based on the alleviation of the plight of those "toiling and unemployed millions who do not even get a square meal a day and have to scratch along with a piece of stale (bread) and pinch of salt."[7] The entire edge of his constructive programme was directed against the poverty of the rural and urban masses. In 1933, he agreed with Nehru that "without a material revision of vested interests the condition of the masses can never be improved," and that "we should range ourselves with the progressive forces of the world."[8] The most remarkable development was his shift towards agrarian radicalism. At the end of 1937, he said:[9]

> Real socialism has been handed down to us by our ancestors who taught: "All land belongs to Gopal, where then is the boundary line? Man is the maker of the line and he can therefore unmake it." Gopal literally means shepherd; it also means God. In modern language it means the State, i.e., the people. That the land today does not belong to the people is too true. But the fault is not in the teaching. It is in us who have not lived up to it. I have no doubt that we can make as good an approach to it as is possible for any nation, not excluding Russia, and that without violence.... Land and all property is his who will work it. Unfortunately the workers are or have been kept ignorant of this simple fact.

[6] Tendulkar, *op. cit.*, Vol. 3, p. 277.
[7] Gandhi, *Socialism of My Conception*, p. 255.
[8] *Collected Works*, Vol. 55, p. 427.
[9] *Ibid.*, Vol. 64, p. 192.

Similarly, in June 1942 Gandhi told Louis Fischer in answer to his question: "What is your programme for the improvement of the lot of the peasantry?" that "the peasants would take the land. We would not have to tell them to take it. They would take it." And when Fischer asked. "Would the landlords be compensated," he replied: "No. That would be fiscally impossible." Fischer asked: "Well, how do you actually see your impending civil disobedience movement?" Gandhi replied: "In the villages, the peasants will stop paying taxes. They will make salt despite official prohibition.... Their next step will be to seize the land." "With violence?" asked Fischer. Gandhi replied: "There may be violence, but then again the landlords may co-operate.... They might cooperate by fleeing." Fischer said that the landlords "might organize violent resistance." Gandhi's reply was: "There may be fifteen days of chaos, but I think we could soon bring that under control." Did this mean, asked Fischer, that there must be "confiscation without compensation?" Gandhi replied: "Of course. It would be financially impossible for anybody to compensate the landlords."[10]

We may also point out that the basic and increasing radical commitment of Gandhi has not been properly understood by historians, as also some of his contemporary radicals, because his idiom was very different from that of the European Liberal-Labour radicals or the Marxists. But his followers had little difficulty in understanding what he was saying. Our interviews with grassroot Gandhian workers show that they followed Gandhi precisely because they saw a socio-economic and political radical in him.[11] In the 1930s and 1940s their major difference with the Socialists and Communists was not regarding their radical economic programme but on the question of non-violence.

[10] *Collected Works*, Vol. 76, pp. 437, 445-6.

[11] For example, interviews with Chhotubhai Gopalji Desai, Puni, Bardoli, Gujarat, 25-6-1985, and Chhotubhai Nathubhai Rathore, Khoj, Bardoli, Gujarat, 24-6-1985. Nehru was another radical who understood this. In his address at Lucknow in March 1936, Nehru feelingly referred to Gandhi's "passionate desire for Indian independence and the raising of our poverty-stricken masses which consumes him." S. Gopal, ed., *Selected Works*, Vol. 7, p. 195.

The pro-poor orientation imparted a dynamic cutting edge to the national movement in the hands of Nehru, Subhas, Socialists, Communists and other left-wing elements who were a powerful, growing and basic constituent of the National Congress in the 1930s.

To sum up: The anti-colonial ideology combined with the vision of a civil libertarian, democratic, secular, socially radical, economically developing, independent and united polity, and the pro-poor radical orientation enabled the Congress to base the national movement on the masses and mass mobilization and to give it the character of a popular, people's movement.

CHAPTER 3

Strategy

A very basic aspect of the dynamics of the national movement was the strategy it adopted in its struggle against colonial rule. The capacity of a people to struggle depends not only on the fact of exploitation and domination and on its comprehension by the people but also on the costs or the people's perception of the costs the struggle might involve and the strategy and tactics on which the struggle is based. Strategy is crucial to the development of the capacity to struggle; and a successful strategy must be, and must appear to be, feasible and effective and based on the capacity of the people to bear the cost.

A focus on the over-all strategy of the Indian national movement has been lacking in almost all the existing studies of the movement, and it might thus appear that the Indian national movement had no strategy at all! We believe, however, that the weakness has been more in the perceptions of the historians than in the practice of the movement. The Indian national movement was not merely a conglomeration of different struggles or an amalgam of pragmatic politics but was based on a specific, though largely unauthorized, strategy of struggle for a basic change in state power; and its various constituent struggles, phases, constitutional activities, constructive work, basic political decisions, forms of struggle, non-violence, etc., were integral parts of this strategy. It is the historian's task, we believe, to bring out and analyze this strategy and its basic elements, etc., and to examine the extent of its adequacy or inadequacy in terms of the achievement of the objectives of the movement.

Though large elements of this strategy were evolved during the Moderate and Extremist phases of the movement, it was structured and came to fruition during the Gandhian phase of the movement and in Gandhi's political practice. We will, therefore, in our discussion on strategy, concentrate basically on this period. And because of Gandhi's dominant position as 'the generalissimo' of the movement, as he often described himself, the spotlight has to be turned on him. Both friends and foes have concentrated on his philosophy of life, but his philosophy of life had only a limited impact—it extended at the most to a few hundred thousand. But it is as a political leader whose political strategy and tactics and techniques of struggle moved millions into political action and were his basic contribution to Indian history—and perhaps world history—that he needs to be studied. Though a brilliant intellectual and thinker and a voluminous writer, he was, unlike his two major contemporaries, Lenin and Mao, not given to detailed theorizing. His strategy and the strategy of the movement he led have therefore to be derived from a study of the actual movement and not from the written word, though sometimes his spoken and written word has shown us the way. For the same reason, our own study is based on the perception of the participants in the struggle via interviews with grassroot, village and *taluka* level political workers as also with some who were already working at the time as district or provincial leaders.

Two more general remarks. The nationalist strategy was based on the logic of the state against which it was directed and on its own logic as a mass movement. It was also the product of the specific history of a people and their psychology. It continuously evolved by critically incorporating the ongoing practice of the movement itself,[1] and

[1]That he was not unaware of the specificity in time and space of his strategy is evident from what Gandhi told a Chinese delegation on the last day of December 1938: "I should love to be able to say to the Chinese definitely that their salvation lay only through non-violent technique. But then it is not for a person like me, who is outside the fight, to say to a

was constantly open to development in response to changes in the adversary's strategy and tactics.[2]

Surprisingly, the contemporary or later left-wing critics of Gandhi have neither made an effort to understand this strategy, nor have they subjected it to a serious critique from the perspective of an alternative strategy. An *effective* critique of Gandhian leadership and its tactics at any specific period of time or its stand on particular political issues could have been made only if the critique extended to and was based on an understanding of the Gandhian strategy. Then alone could its strong and weak points have been understood and its historical effectivity seriously challenged or accepted. The neo-colonial historians also do not recognize the existence of any strategic perspective in the national movement for the simple reason that their historiographic framework does not recognize the Indian national movement as a mass movement or 'war' against colonialism. Further, since they believe that the political initiative throughout emanated from the British, and the nationalists at each stage did nothing but respond to it, they cannot possibly conceive of the national movement as having a strategic design of its own.

II

The nationalist strategy was based on a particular understanding of the specific nature and character of British rule and the colonial state and its policies. First of all, as we have already shown, the exploitative and dominational aspect of colonialism was fully grasped. But it was also realized that the colonial state was semi-hegemonic, semi-authoritarian in character. It was not like Hitler's Germany, or Tsarist Russia, or Chiang Kai-shek's China, or Batista's

people who are engaged in a life-and-death struggle, 'Not this way, but that.' They would not be ready to take up the new method, and they would be unsettled in the old. My interference would only shake them and confuse their minds." *Collected Works,* Vol. 68, p. 262.

[2] *Ibid.,* Vol. 69, p. 60.

Cuba, or Samoza's Nicaragua, or Portuguese Mozambique, or even French Algeria or Vietnam. Its character could perhaps be best described as legal authoritarianism. The colonial state was simultaneously hegemonic and suppressive, civil and 'semi-fascist.'

The colonial state was established by force and force remained its ultimate sanction—the mailed fist beneath the glove—and was often used. It took recourse to naked force and repression—sometimes savage—when faced with peaceful mass movements. Lakhs bore the marks of its brutal lathi-charges and thousands of its sometimes barbarous treatment in jails—for example, public whipping on the naked back or buttocks with leather thongs for breach of jail rules.

But it was not based just on force. It was also based on the creation of certain civil institutions and on the rule of law, a certain amount of civil liberties, and a certain toleration of, and civil behaviour towards, its opponents. Even while suppressing, it observed certain rules of law and codes of administration.[3] In other words, it was semi-democratic.

Moreover, it relied very heavily for the acquiescence of the people on the twin ideologies of the rulers being benevolent and just and their rule being permanent and invincible. The notion of benevolence was purveyed through the ideology of the British being the *Mai-Baap* of the people, of protecting India from external aggressors, of having established law and order and provided stable and equitable administration after centuries of anarchy, despotism and arbitrary justice and taxation, of being the defenders of private property against anarchy and confiscation, of acting as the fair and even—handed arbiters between warring Indian groups and communities even while protecting the weaker ones, of having established equality

[3]For example, when confiscating peasant property during the Bardoli Satyagraha in 1928 or the no tax campaign in Kheda during 1930, the police would not enter houses after dark or break into locked houses; nor would officials seize or confiscate food stuffs when people in the village refused to sell these to them. Cf H.V.R. Iyengar, I.C.S., *Oral History Transcript*, NMML.

before law between the rich and the poor and the high caste and low caste, of giving protection to peasants from predatory landlords and moneylenders, to workers from greedy capitalists, to women from oppressive males, and above all of economically developing India and removing the poverty of its people. The colonial state also widely propagated the view that it was invincible and that it was not possible to oppose or challenge it except in the space and through channels that it provided, and that it would, on its own, continuously widen the space and provide more and more channels for the purpose.

There were certain other hegemonic features of the colonial state, which it shared with democratic politics, such as continuous effort to create channels, institutions and opportunities for co-option of its opponents, and to offer constitutional, economic and other concessions to popular movements and ameliorative measures to the discontented and not rely only on their suppression through naked force when use of such force could become counter productive or even impossible in certain situations because of erosion of hegemony. These and other similar features would be discussed in the course of our analysis of the nationalist strategy.

A few other comments may be made at this stage. One reason why the colonial state in India acquired a hegemonic character was that the British at home had a democratic government which had to justify the policies and behaviour of its agents in India to the British people. The liberal-radical trend in the 19th century and the emergence of powerful anti-imperialist sentiments in the ranks of trade unions and Labour Party in the 20th made greater reliance on hegemonic instruments and ideology even more imperative just at a time when the rise of a powerful national movement was making resort to coercive instruments more necessary. The colonial state and its policies had also to accommodate and provide room for the sensitivities of the British colonial bureaucrats, who were socialized in public schools that trained them not to hit a man when he was down and out or when he did not resist and in universities that taught liberal and humanist values, and were in general products of a civil and democratic polity.

Rule through naked force was also perhaps ruled out because of its non-viability in a country of India's size and population, especially in view of Britain's own size and distance from India, and the relatively small number of British administrative personnel and British troops in India.[4] At the same time, the colonial state in India was a strong or hard state. It had considerable force at its command. Whenever needed, it had the capacity, except perhaps near the end, to deploy effective force.

The semi-hegemonic and 'civil' character of British rule and its difference from regimes based on naked force was fully perceived by the nationalists. Most of our interviewees, even those who had been brutally lathi-charged or have spent years in jail, pointed to this aspect. Several women freedom fighters, especially in Andhra and Gujarat where the level of women's participation in the freedom movement was phenomenal, told us that what enabled them to go to jail or persuaded their families to let them do so was the knowledge and/or feeling that the police would not misbehave towards them. Many interviewees said that a non-violent struggle could not have been waged against Hitler or the Tsar. A few pointed out that peaceful struggle failed even against the Portuguese in Goa—the Indian army had in the end to march in. A large number of nationalists and ex-civil servants whom we interviewed saw the peaceful transfer of power in 1947 as the logical consequence of the British realization that they could no longer continue to rule on the old basis and their unwillingness to prolong their stay by changing the basis of their rule to one that relied primarily on force and uncivil forms of rule.[5]

[4]British policy in this respect was quite different in some of the smaller colonies of Africa and Asia.

[5]The freedom fighters who made this point are too many to be cited here. Among the I.C.S., S.R. Kaiwar (Madras, 2-6-84) and R.A. Gopalaswamy (Madras, 5-6-84) emphasized this aspect most strongly.

Gandhi too was fully aware of the semi-hegemonic, semi-suppressive character of British rule. He wrote in *Harijan* of 4 September 1937: "British domination of India has been on the whole a curse. It has been as much sustained by British arms as it has been through the legislatures, distribution of titles, the law-courts, the educational institutions, the financial policy and the like."[6] In the *Harijan* of 23 April 1938, he wrote: "The Congress has only moral authority to back it. The ruling power has the martial, though it often dilutes the martial with the moral."[7] In the same month, while dealing with the political crisis in Orissa, he referred to "the prestige of autocracy" which "depended upon its exacting obedience, willing or unwilling, from the ruled."[8] On 6 August, with reference to the crisis in the Central Provinces, he wrote in the *Harijan:* "Democratic Britain has set up an ingenious system in India which, when you look at it in its nakedness, is nothing but a highly organized efficient military control."[9] Gandhi's understanding of the character of the colonial state and its points of convergence as well as divergence from purely authoritarian states emerged clearly in his comments on the Princely States during 1938-39, especially when he explained why the Congress could not intervene there directly and why it would be more difficult as well as require great resources of political will, sacrifice and mass mobilization to wage Congress-type movements and campaigns there. For example, in the context of the Haripura resolution on the States, in 1938, he explained to a group of political workers why it was possible for the Congress to defend the honour of the Congress flag in British India but not in the States: "In British India we can adopt civil disobedience for any good cause, but in the States it is impossible. The Congress Committees will have always to be at the mercy of the States and would be in no better case than, for instance, a Committee in Afghanistan, which would entirely exist on

[6] *Collected Works,* Vol. 66, p. 104.
[7] *Ibid,* Vol. 67, p. 39.
[8] *Ibid,* p. 52.
[9] *Ibid.,* p. 226.

the mercy of the Government of Afghanistan."[10] At the height of his struggle against the colonial state in 1942, Gandhi on the one hand referred to the "powerful elements of Fascism in British rule" and on the other hand to the "fundamental difference between Fascism and even this imperialism which I am fighting."[11]

It was in the context of and in opposition to this semi-hegemonic, semi-authoritarian colonial state that the national movement gradually evolved its strategy and tactics. We may point out in this context that strategy and tactics depend less on the class character of the movement and more on the political structure or character of the state to be overthrown. For example, the Taiping peasants, semi-feudal warlords, bourgeois democratic Sun yat-sen, Chiang Kai-shek, the leader of the compradore bourgeoisie and landlords, and the leaders of workers and peasants, the Communists, all followed the strategy of armed struggle in China, though the class character of their movements varied greatly. Similar was the case with the nationalist revolts in Poland, Ireland, Italy and virtually all of Latin America in the 19th century and Turkey, etc., in the 20th.

III

(i) The war of position required 'a far more complex political struggle,' a specific combination of forms of struggle in which the political element would always prevail over the military. A typical example of this war of position was the anti-colonialist resistance of Gandhi in India, the boycott movement as preparation for a further stage. In this case, there are 'forms of mixed struggle-fundamentally of a military character, but mainly fought on the

[10] *Ibid.,* Vol. 66, pp. 391-2. Among other things, the Haripura resolution had said: "In view of the different conditions prevailing in the states and the rest of India, the general policy of the Congress is often unsuited to the States...." In Tendulkar, *op. cit.,* Vol. 4, p. 223.

[11] *Collected Works,* Vol. 76, pp. 439 and 400 respectively.

political plane.' To take a different historical example, outside Gramsci's own experience, we could define the war of position as a 'strategy of long-term resistance,' in General Giap's formulation, a people's war in which it is 'necessary to accumulate thousands of small victories to turn them into a great success.'

However different the struggle in Vietnam, this is not so foreign to the spirit of Gramsci's thinking. In his analysis of Gandhi's resistance movement, Gramsci stressed that 'this type of struggle is suitable for a country that is technically disarmed and militarily inferior, being dominated by technically developed and superior countries.' At the start, 'the consciousness of material impotence on the part of a great mass confronts a minority of oppressors.' The situation is favourable for a 'war of position.' A 'long-term' struggle of this kind starts from a situation of imbalance, in which the enemy is stronger. But it seeks to change this situation in stages (defensive phase, relative equilibrium, counter-offensive).

The necessary build-up of forces, this celebrated 'unprecedented concentration of hegemony,' is not simply confined to an assault on the enemy's 'trenches.' It also requires 'a large mass of people: the struggle of a people.' This is why it is impossible without 'accurate reconnaissance of each individual country.'

It required a reconnaissance of the terrain and identification of the elements of trench and fortress represented by the elements of civil society.

To translate these points into a strategic doctrine, war of position, as a long-term strategy, proceeds by an unprecedented siege of the principal and secondary contradictions specific to the society in question. Basing itself on the masses and their organizations, this is for Gramsci the only possible strategy in the developed capitalist countries of the West; hence its double class character. (Christine Buci-Glucksmann, *Gramsci and the State,* pp. 251-52).

> (ii) Thus India's political struggle against the English ... knows three forms of war: war of movement, war of position and under ground warfare. Gandhi's passive resistance is a war of position, which at certain moments becomes a war of movement, and at others underground warfare. Boycotts are a form of war of position, strikes of war of movement, the secret preparation of weapons and combat troops belongs to underground warfare. (Antonio Gramsci, *Prison Notebooks,* pp. 229-30).

The basic strategic perspective of the Indian National Congress was to wage a long-drawn out hegemonic struggle or in Gramscian terms a war of position—a struggle for the minds and hearts of men and women, constantly expanding its influence among the people through different channels and its different movements and phases or stages. This strategy had two basic thrusts. It was hegemonic and it alternated between phases of extra legal mass struggle and phases of truce functioning within the four walls of the law or in Gramscian terms between phases of war of manoeuvre and war of position. But both phases were geared to expanding the influence of the national movement among the people. The basic strategy was the same, but the tactics differed in different phases and over time. It was, moreover, not a strategy of gradual reform or 'compromise' with colonialism or of seeking co-option into it or of 'sharing' power and privileges with it. It was a strategy of active struggle by building reserves of hegemonic power with a view to wresting political power from the colonial state. Even though it represented an alternative not only to the path of armed struggle but in many ways also to the Leninist strategic framework, it shared with the latter a common strategic objective, the capture of state power.

The entire effectiveness and validity of the strategy and the strength of the movement based on it lay in the active participation of the masses. They had, therefore, to be politicized, activised and brought into politics. The political passivity of the masses, especially in the villages, consciously inculcated and nurtured by the colonial

the counter-hegemonic movement to expose it to the light of the day. In basically non-hegemonic societies, the face of the enemy is clear or soon becomes clear once mass political work is seriously taken up, and how to fight the enemy, that is, the material resources of strength or war, become the crucial element. In hegemonic societies, it is the ideological influence, its reach and depth, that matters. Hence the most important element of nationalist strategy was its ideological-political work.

Above all, this meant undermining the twin notions of the benevolence and invincibility of British rule. The process of undermining the first and creating an intellectual framework for it was initiated and performed brilliantly by Dadabhai Naoroji and other Moderates. This framework was carried to the middle classes by the Extremists and to the masses during the Gandhian era both by the Gandhians and the Left. The invincibility of the colonial state was frontally challenged by the nationalist Press, since the 1870s, by the bold stance adopted by Pherozeshah Mehta, G.K. Gokhale and others in the legislative councils, and by Tilak and the Extremists and the Revolutionary Terrorists. But it was the law-breaking mass movements of the post-1918 period which basically performed the task among the mass of the Indian people. These movements were basically hegemonic (even when wars of manoeuvre) because at no stage were they geared to the seizure of power. Their basic objective or thrust as well as achievement was to destroy the notion that British rule could not be challenged, to create among the people fearlessness and courage and the capacity to fight and make sacrifices, to inculcate the notion that no people could be ruled without their consent and that it was their duty as well as right to resist 'tyranny,' exploitation, and 'a ruler who misrules,' and to demonstrate to the British authorities as well as British public opinion the growing acceptance of nationalist ideology by the Indian people.

The objective of creating fearlessness was the major reason why Gandhi opposed any recourse to secret methods even during the illegal phases of the movement.[17] The hegemonic struggle also required immense faith in the people's capacity to struggle. It was also above all a moral battle, a contest in moral force and fibre. That is why the national leaders from Naoroji to Gandhi always stood on high moral ground, demanding and standing by public enquiries into all their critiques of colonialism and colonial politics and their allegations against the acts of the colonial bureaucracy. Nearly all the major movements were taken up around strong moral issues rather than on mere political or economic demands: the Rowlatt Bills in 1919, the Panjab wrongs and breach of faith on the Khilafat question in 1920-22, the salt tax which was more a moral than an economic wrong in 1930, the pre-emptive strike against the national leaders and movement in 1932, India being made a party to the war without her consent in 1939, the failure to defend India and implement the high principles around which the war was being fought in 1942, and the release of patriotic Indian soldiers and officers of the INA in 1945. The Gandhian-era non-violent movements consistently counterpoised their moral authority to the rulers' combined moral and physical force.[18] The question of the moral legitimacy of the movement as well as its moral superiority over the regime was always at the centre of all nationalist movements.

[17]For example, Gandhi in a letter to Nehru on 14 September, 1933: "There may be exceptional circumstances that may warrant secret methods. I would forgo that advantage for the sake of the masses whom we want to educate in fearlessness.... Secrecy is inimical to the growth of the spirit of civil resistance." *Collected Works,* Vol. 55, p. 429. During the 1930 and 1932-34 movements, the workers were permitted to remain underground in the sense of not being available for arrest. But they were not permitted to give a false name to anyone, including to a policeman whom they might come across or to give up wearing Khadi—'the livery of freedom' but also an open mark of identification. Based on our interviews.

[18]The feeling that the Congress was getting tainted with nepotism and corruption was responsible for Gandhi being 'in slough of despond' during early 1939 and for his strong view in opposition to that of Subhas Bose and the Left that the country was not yet ready for another round of mass, extra-legal struggle. See Gyanesh Kudaisya, *Office Acceptance and the Congress 1937-1939: Premises and Perceptions,* Chapter 7, M. Phil. dissertation.

A third objective of Congress strategy was to undermine the hold of the colonial state on the members of its own state apparatuses, destroy their morale, promote 'rebelliousness' among them, and to neutralize or win them over to the nationalist cause.[19] This task was not so difficult in the case of Indian members of the bureaucracy, since as members of a subject nation they were inevitably open to a nationalist appeal, but it was undertaken with some success even in the case of its British members by adopting a civil behaviour and a non-racial non-hatred approach towards them.[20] "The British system was wooden, even Satanic," wrote Gandhi in *Harijan* in September 1937, "not so the men and women behind the system. Our non-violence, therefore, meant that we were out to convert the administrators of the system, not to destroy them...."[21] The national movement was quite successful in this task. Partly as a result of its hegemonic politics, and partly because of the Congress occupying offices in 1937 and the prospects of a repeat performance after the war, the behaviour of the police and jail officials underwent a qualitative change during 1940-45.[22] A large number of officials of all types actively helped the 1942 movement at great risk.[23] And, of course, the virtual disappearance of loyalty among the police, army and bureaucracy after 1945 is well-known and was a major reason

[19]One reason why the Government of India was keen to reverse the political line that had led to the Gandhi-Irwin Pact and go over to a policy of firmness in dealing with the Congress was the fear of the loss of its hegemony over its own functionaries, especially village officials and police. See R.J. Moore, *The Crisis of Indian Unity*, p. 289.

[20]An interesting incident of the impact of this approach on a British police official in 1942 was recounted by Sarla Devi Mazumdar (Bombay, 29-5-1985).

[21]*Collected Works*, Vol. 66, p. 104.

[22]See, for example, M. Hallett's note on the Satyagraha Movement, 22 April 1941, *Linlithgow Papers*, F. 125/104.

[23]Achyut Patwardhan (Bangalore, 7-12-1984) told us that one of the three members of the team of top officials deputed to control the 1942 movement in Bombay actively helped the nationalists. Some of the large number who had similar stories to tell about the 1942 movement are Lata Povaiah (Bombay, 21-5-85), Vasantdada Patil (Bombay, 14-6-1985), Anavathukkal Achuthan (Kasargod, Kerala, 13-5-1984).

for the British decision to finally quit India.[24] In fact one could draw a linear upward moving curve of the attitude of the police and other officials towards the national movement and the Satyagrahis from 1920 to 1945.

The national movement, from the beginning, made efforts to weaken the hegemony of colonial ideology among the British people and public opinion. This as well as efforts to win the support of non-Congress leaders and public opinion within India were also essential for the achievement of a fourth objective of the strategy: to constantly expand the semi-democratic space, and prevent the colonial authorities from limiting the existing space, within which legal activities and peaceful mass struggles could be organized.

IV

The second major aspect of nationalist strategy was the long drawn-out character of the hegemonic struggle based on alternation between two different types of phases. Under the Gandhian strategy, whose roots lie in the Moderate and Extremist phases, and which may be described as Struggle—Truce—Struggle′ (S—T—S′),[25] phases of a vigorous extra-legal mass movement and open confrontation with colonial authority alternate with phases during which direct confrontation was withdrawn, political concessions or reforms, if any, wrested from the colonial regime were willy-nilly worked and shown to be inadequate, and intense political and ideological work carried on among the masses within the existing legal and constitutional framework, which, in turn, provided scope

[24]For a discussion of the disarray of the British administrative structure in the last phase of British rule, and its impact on the decision to leave India, see Sucheta Mahajan, "British Policy and the Popular National Upsurge, 1945-46," in A.K. Gupta, ed., *Myth and Reality—Struggle for Freedom, 1945-47.*

[25]I have earlier in 1972 described this strategy as Pressure-Compromise-Pressure (P-C-P'). I was at the time trying to make the initial break with the existing Marxian analysis and was therefore not able to get rid of all the cobwebs. Prolonged discussion with my colleagues has, I hope, improved the understanding, though it is still in-the-making, so to speak.

for such work; forces were gathered for another mass movement at a higher level till finally a call for 'quit India' was given and the ultimate concession of independence was extracted. Both phases of the movement were to be utilized, each in its own way, to undermine colonial hegemony and to recruit and train cadre and to build up the people's capacity to struggle. The entire political process of S-T-S′ was an upward spiralling one, which also assumed that the freedom struggle would pass through several stages, ending with the transfer of power by the colonial regime itself. An old participant, Madhavlal Shankarlal Pandya, a village and *taluka* level leader of Borsad, Kheda, Gujarat, put this strategy in his own colourful words: *Lado* (struggle)—*Jo Mile So Lo* (take what is given) (it is the product of our struggle, he said)—*Bhogo* (utilize it) (but for people and not for self, he said)—*Phir Lado* (fight again).[26]

This strategy assumed advance through stages but the stages were stages of the freedom struggle and not of freedom. Freedom was a whole; till it was fully won, it was not won at all. Freedom could not be won "bit by bit," or by "two annas or four annas," as Nehru put it.[27] The constitutional concessions from 1892, 1907, 1919, 1935 to 1946 were to be accepted as the fruits of the freedom struggle itself, but they were not to be seen as half or one-fourth of freedom. Each stage represented an advance over the previous one, but this fact was not to permit one to blunt the notion that the task of national liberation was incomplete and that state power as such was still with the other side and would remain so till the last act of transfer of power. Hence working the reforms was not to be equated with working the system; the movement was not to let itself be co-opted.[28] In fact, a basic strategic task was to move from stage to stage

[26]Interview, Piplav, Kheda, Gujarat, 3-7-1985.

[27]Either imperialism would retain power or the Indians would take possession "of the citadel," Nehru added. *Selected Works,* Vol. 6, p. 104.

[28]We might say that this and not participating in parliaments or forming governments was the crucial mistake that the Social Democratic Parties made in Europe in the 1920s.

without getting co-opted. Nor were the phases of non-mass movement phases of non-politics or non-struggle. Only the form of struggle changed in these phases from civil disobedience and breaking of laws to mass agitation and intense ideological work, including extensive tours by leaders, organization of public meetings on an extensive scale, etc.

Nor was the non-mass movement phase the primary one. It was in fact only the preparatory ground for the mass movement phase, which was seen as the prime mover in the overall war. The leadership was always keen to shorten the time-gap between two waves of mass struggle.[29] But the decision could not be a subjective one. It depended on the organization, political and ideological preparedness of the people. Furthermore, both type of phases were to be seen as political phases of the same movement, equally rich in anti-imperialist content, and parts of the same anti-imperialist strategy. They were not dichotomous, one a phase of compromise with (if not surrender before) imperialism and the other a phase of struggle against it. Political struggle was perpetual, only its forms underwent change. As Gandhi put it, "suspension of civil disobedience does not mean suspension of war. The latter can only end when India has a Constitution of her own making."[30] A little later, he said: "In satyagraha there is no such thing as disappointment or heart-burning. The struggle always goes on in some shape or other till the goal is reached. A satyagrahi is indifferent whether it is civil disobedience or some other phase of the struggle to which he is called. Nor does he mind if, in the middle of the civil disobedience march, he is called upon to halt and do something else."[31]

Many a contemporary Congress leader clearly understood the S-T-S′ aspects of the strategy and the relationship between the 'active'

[29]One reason why Gandhi promoted Nehru as the front-ranking leader of the Congress in 1935-36 was his keenness to go over to the mass movement phase as soon as possible.

[30]*Collected Works,* Vol. 67, p. 226.

[31]*Ibid.,* Vol. 69, pp. 78-9.

and 'passive' phases. For example, Acharya Kripalani, General Secretary of the Congress, told an audience at Vizagapatnam in 1935:[32]

> We tried and found that constitutional action through toy Councils gave nothing substantial. We could not wrest power from government through prayer, protest or petitions. But we cannot always be fighting. Reading history, we find that every nation in its struggle for freedom has had periods of comparative quietness—periods in which they consolidate gains and gather fresh strength. So also here it is not possible for the nation to put forth at all times sufficient energy and sacrifice to carry on the fight to a finish. To a superficial observer it might appear that we have abandoned the fight, but a national fight cannot be abandoned until the national aim is achieved. We are waiting for another uprising of the nation's spirit. A nation is like the sea. It has got its ebb and flow. We cannot artificially create a tide and we cannot go forward during the ebb. We started the non-cooperation movement in 1921 and had to wait till 1930 for another effort. We are gathering strength and waiting for another inflow of national spirit.

At the Lucknow session of the Congress, he said:[33]

> We cannot lose sight of the fact that we are in the grip of depression. This should not mean we should not do little things because at present the spirit of doing great things is not in us. We are just like an army in barracks. What does such an army do? All its activity appears peaceful, tame, sometime even useless. The soldiers dig trenches that they fill up the next day, they go on big marches that go nowhere, they shoot at targets without killing.

[32]*AICC News Letter*, Letter No. 31, 14 November 1935. D.K. Kunte pointed out that even in Russia the revolution of 1905 was followed by 12 years of comparative quiet. Interview, Pune, 6-6-1985.

[33]J.B. Kripalani, Speech at Lucknow Congress, in A.M. and S.G. Zaidi, editors, *The Encyclopaedia of Indian National Congress*, Vol. 11, p. 48.

All this to the untrained eye has no value and leads nowhere but to the trained military eye, all this drilling, digging, marching and shooting, however apparently useless, is a necessary part of preparation of war. If this was neglected, no army would be fit to fight. Even in a revolutionary movement, there may be times of comparative depression and inactivity. At such times, whatever programmes are devised have necessarily an appearance of reformatory activity but they are all a necessary part of all revolutionary strategy.

K.M. Munshi, another leader of the movement, expressed his understanding of its dynamics thus:[34]

> The history of the Congress during the last thirty years shows how this strength has grown out of the rhythmic movements of our national life. A lull has followed the storm and in its turn has been followed by a still more powerful storm. Every succeeding upheaval has been characterized by an increasing wider basis and sterner resistance. This was achieved by the Congress, not by shouting impossible slogans or making impatient gestures, but by acquiring a wider control over the life of the people during every period of lull. The real object of the Congress, therefore, is to prepare the country for a new life by gaining greater control over all forms of social organization, governmental and non-governmental.

V

A basic question regarding the S-T-S′ strategy is: why did there have to be two types of phases in the movement? Why should a phase of war of position inevitably follow a phase of war of movement? Why could not there be one continuous struggle or the strategy be that of Struggle-Victory (S-V) as the left, including Nehru, urged between

[34]K.M. Munshi, 'Office Acceptance: A Survey of the Problem,' Pamphlet, *Rajendra Prasad Papers*, File No. 1/36, Collection 6.

1933-37?[35] In finding an answer, we have relied heavily on the collective wisdom of the participants as it has emerged in our interviews. There has been a virtual consensus on the answer among the lower-level, village-*taluka* cadre or political workers, whether belonging to the left, right or Gandhian currents, who actually organized the mass *Satyagraha* movements at the grassroot level.

The Gandhian strategy was based on the assumptions that by its very nature a mass movement could not be carried on or sustained indefinitely or even for a prolonged period, that a mass movement must ebb sooner or later, that no mass movement could be on the rise permanently, that mass movements had to be short-lived, and that periods of rest and consolidation, of 'breathing time,' must intervene so that the movement could consolidate, recuperate and gather strength for the next round of struggle.

And why was this so? Because the masses involved in the movement invariably got exhausted after some time. Their capacity to confront the state or to face state repression—imprisonment, lathi-charges (often brutal), heavy fines, auction and confiscation of property—or to endure suffering, especially that of their old parents, wives and children, or make sacrifices was (and is) not unlimited. Despite awareness of long-term interests, consciousness of exploitation and impoverishment, and ideological commitment to nationalism, people might not engage in battle beyond a certain point because of the high costs involved. The answer would be to continuously increase their capacity to sacrifice and bear the cost

[35]The left believed that the national movement should have a permanent mass and extra-legal confrontation and conflict with imperialism till it was overthrown. The movement might suffer setbacks and phases of upswing and downswing but these should not lead to a passive phase where open confrontation is withdrawn, some of the colonial institutions worked, and energy diverted to the non-political and non-class constructive programme. In the words of Nehru, the Congress must maintain "an aggressive direct action policy." The nationalist mass struggle must become perpetual and could go forward only through unconstitutional and illegal means. Once the masses enter and take over a movement, no half-way house is left.

through ideological motivation, and simultaneously recognize the limits of their capacity to bear the cost and not strain this capacity overmuch.[36] It should also be seen that a strong state, a state that is not in disarray, has a considerable capacity to crush a movement as was done by using strong measures by the Willingon regime in 1932-33 and 'leonine violence' by the Linlithgow administration in 1942.

It was not only the property-owning middle classes that had a limited capacity to bear the cost. The land-owning peasants including the smallest ones were even more open to political blackmail by the state in the form of loss of land. In 1932, the peasant-participants in the civil disobedience movement were readily suppressed, except in a few brave pockets, when their lands and property were sold by the government at throw away prices to recover fines and collect taxes. The agricultural and urban day labourers and their families, who depended almost entirely on their daily earnings, not only could not sustain a movement for long, they found it difficult to even participate in the law-breaking jail-going part of it. After all, a peasant had a brother or a tenant to cultivate his land, a middle-class person or landlord or a middle peasant had some financial reserve or family backing; a day labourer and his family would starve if the bread earner was absent from work for any length of time. We may point out that this perception regarding the capacity

[36]As Madhavlal Shankarlal Pandya put it (Interview, Piplav, Kheda, Gujarat, 3-7-1985), the masses get tired, take rest, and then go forward. He also said that they could not withstand too much repression. D.K. Kunte also made the same point (Interview, Pune, 6-6-1985). He recounted the incident which opened his eyes to this aspect of the people's incapacity to undertake prolonged struggle. He was, like many other young men, unhappy over the withdrawal of the movement following the Gandhi-Irwin Pact in 1931. En route to the Karachi session of the Congress, he addressed a public meeting and in the course of his speech he gave vent to his feeling of disappointment at the calling off of the movement. When he sat down, a man in peasant dress came forward to speak, and addressing Kunte, asked: "Are you married?" Kunte said, "No." "Do you have a father who supports you?" "Yes." "That explains your readiness to carry on with the struggle. If you had a family of your own and had to feed them, you would talk a very different tune." Ganga Saran Sinha, one of the founders of the Bihar Socialist Party in 1931 (Interview, New Delhi, 15-12-1985), and many others have argued the same position in their interviews.

of the masses to bear repression does not reflect the chicken-heartedness of middle class or 'bourgeois' leaders whom we interviewed. For one, this view is shared by left-wing political workers as well. What is more important, the cadre interviewed were those who had devoted their life till 1947—and often even after—to the nationalist cause. They were the whole timers of the national movement, except that they got no party wage. They, as thousands of others like them, did wage perpetual struggle and did face state repression and loss of hearth and home most heroically. They made life long sacrifices. Many took a vow not to marry till freedom's day. They sat all their lives in jails, or Ashrams, or Khadi Bhavans, or in trade union and Kisan Sabha offices, or, like Nehru, never sat at home but perambulated all over the land the year round. They were the 'standing army'[37] of the national movement. Only, they, as also Gandhi and the Congress leaders, felt that a mass movement could not be waged by a 'standing army,' however important their role in organizing and mobilizing the masses might be. In fact, it was felt that a movement based on a 'standing army' would rapidly tend to lose its mass character.[38]

Thus, to sum up, withdrawal or a shift to a phase of non-confrontation vis-a-vis the state and its laws was bound to be an inherent part of a strategy of political action that was based on the masses, except in the case of the final stage when, in Gramscian terms, the citadel is stormed or occupied or, as Gandhi visualized, power is transferred. Gandhi understood this for he knew the limits to which both the people and the Government could go, and he worked out his strategy and tactics accordingly.

[37]The phrase is D.K. Kunte's. Interview, *op. cit.*

[38]See, for example, D.K. Kunte, Interview, *op. cit.* Most of the guerilla type activists in the 1942 movement, both right wing and left wing, were very clear that they were not substitutes for a mass movement. They saw the underground activities as mainly performing the task of keeping up the morale of the masses. (See, e.g., Achyut Patwardhan, *op. cit.*) Some, however, later argued that it was a mistake to fall into the easier path of underground activity; the attempt should have remained one of trying to build up a mass movement, however difficult and limited it might have been in that context. See, for example, Lalbhai Dahyabhai Naik, Interview, Navsari, Gujarat, 27-6-1985.

Because the critics of the Gandhian leadership have not seen a strategic design, to which tactics of the movement were subordinated, they have looked for sources of decisions regarding withdrawals in class bias or essence, class pressure, betrayal, tendency to compromise with imperialism, loss of nerve, moral compunction, etc., and not in the strategic design itself. But seen from within the strategic perspective of a war of position, withdrawal becomes an inevitable part of the strategy itself. Satyagraha must end in withdrawal or a negotiated compromise; but the manner and timing of its termination is as important as that of its launching and requires as much political skill.

Within the S-T-S′ strategic perspective, the decision to shift from one phase to the other becomes a tactical one: was it in keeping with the reality on the ground? For example, in 1933, Gandhi assured Nehru that the decision to suspend the movement was dictated by the reality of the political situation. But this did not mean following a policy of drift or bowing down before political opportunists or compromising with imperialism. The new policy, he said, "is founded upon one central idea that of consolidating the power of the people."[39] Moreover, he told Nehru in August 1934 regarding the decision to withdraw the movement, "I fancy that I have the knack for knowing the need of the time. And the resolutions are a response thereto."[40] Giving an inkling of his decision-making process, Gandhi wrote in his *Autobiography* that, in the Kheda Satyagraha in 1918, finding that some of the peasants were cowed down by the Government's policy of attaching their cattle, other movables, and standing crops, and were paying their land revenue and that they were "exhausted," he "hesitated to let the unbending be driven to utter ruin" and had begun "casting about for some graceful way of terminating the struggle."[41] Similarly, in a rare analysis of the political

[39] *Collected Works,* Vol. 61, p. 439.
[40] *Ibid.,* Vol. 58, p. 318.
[41] *An Autobiography,* pp. 364-6.

situation at the time of the withdrawal of the Non-Cooperation Movement in early 1922, he wrote in July 1938: "When the fight for swaraj became prolonged and Khilafat ceased to be a live issue, enthusiasm began to wane, confidence in non-violence even as a policy began to be shaken, and untruth crept in. People who had no faith in the twin virtues or the Khadi clause stole in, and many even openly defied the Congress constitution."[42] But perhaps his best theorisation of the issue of withdrawal of movements, and the role of leadership in that context, was made in two statements in 1938 and 1939: "A wise general does not wait till he is actually routed; he withdraws in time in an orderly manner from a position which he knows he would not be able to hold." And: "An able general always gives battle in his own time on the ground of his choice. He always retains the initiative in these respects and never allows it to pass into the hands of the enemy. In a satyagraha campaign the mode of fight and the choice of tactics, e.g., whether to advance or retreat, offer civil resistance or organize non-violent strength through constructive work and purely selfless humanitarian service, are determined according to the exigencies of the situation."[43]

What we wish to emphasize is that a critique of the national movement which merely holds up each act of withdrawal of the movement as proof of betrayal, without making this criticism a part of a more general critique of the entire strategic perspective of the movement of which these withdrawals were an inherent part, is no critique at all. On the other hand, those who accept the basic strategic perspective of the movement must still evaluate whether each withdrawal or retreat was correct in the manner and timing of its execution. So far as the leadership of the actual movement was concerned, it had to decide the question at any point of time on the basis of its perception of the strength or weakness of the movement, the staying power of the masses and the political reserves of the

[42] *Collected Works*, Vol. 67, p. 195

[43] *Ibid.*, p. 420 and Vol. 69, p. 60.

Government. Similarly, the question was not whether negotiations with the Government should or should not be held. The question was, when one negotiated, did one negotiate at the right psychological moment, how one negotiated, what one negotiated about, what was the outcome of the negotiations, and what were the terms on which a truce was signed in case there was a truce.[44]

VI

Constructive work played an important role in the Gandhian strategy. It was primarily organized around the promotion of Khadi, spinning, and village industries, national education and Hindu-Muslim unity, struggle against untouchability and social uplift of the Harijans, and boycott of foreign cloth and liquor. Above all it meant going to villages and identifying with villagers. Constructive work was symbolized by hundreds of Ashrams which came up all over the country, almost entirely in the villages, and in which social and political workers got practical training in production of Khadi and yarn and in work among lower castes and tribal people.

Constructive work was basic to a war of position. It played a crucial role during the 'passive phase' in filling the political space left

[44]The AICC resolution on Congress Policy, adopted on 22 September 1945, stated: "The method of negotiation and conciliation which is the key-note of peaceful policy can never be abandoned by the Congress, no matter how grave may be the provocation, any more than can that of non-cooperation, complete or modified. Hence the guiding maxim of the Congress must remain: negotiations and settlement when possible and non-cooperation and direct action when necessary." *Indian National Congress, March 1940 to September 1946: Being the Resolutions Passed by the Congress, the AICC and the Working Committee,* published by the General Secretary, AICC. This was expressed clearly by Gandhi in 1939: "The first and the last work of a satyagrahi is ever to seek an opportunity for an honourable approach.... Our aim must remain what it is, but we must be prepared to negotiate for less than the whole so long as it is unmistakably of the same kind and has in it inherent possibility of expansion." *Collected Works,* Vol. 69, p. 323. Kripalani emphasized this in his Presidential Address at Meerut, 26 November 1946: "But a satyagrahi is slow to fight and quick to come to terms when he sees an opportunity for a peaceful and honourable solution. If his fundamentals are conceded, he is willing to sit at the table with his opponents to discuss matters." *Presidential Address, Indian National Congress, Fifty-Fourth Session.*

vacant by the withdrawal of civil disobedience, thus solving a basic problem that a mass movement faces, i.e., how to sustain a sense of activism in the non-mass movement phases of the struggle? Withdrawal of a movement tended to generate a sense of despair and depression. The political activists could no longer get sustenance from the mass enthusiasm and exhilaration that a mass movement generated. One answer was found in constructive work, for while mass movements were sporadic, constructive work was to be carried on all the time. Especially for those who had no taste for parliamentary activity, it provided an alternative of continuous and effective work. Gandhi could therefore write with a degree of confidence in 1935: "I am told that there is despair and depression everywhere, that there is disappointment all round as the gateway to jail is closed. People, I am told, do not know what to do. I do not know why, when there is the whole of the constructive programme of work to do."[45]

Constructive work had also the advantage of involving a large number of people. Parliamentary and intellectual work could be done by relatively few, constructive work could involve millions.[46] Moreover, for a variety of reasons, not all could go to jail. But constructive work was within the reach of anyone who was desirous of contributing his mite to the cause of the country.[47]

[45] *Collected Works*, Vol. 61, pp. 88-9.

[46] Tendulkar, *op.cit.*, Vol. 4, p. 44.

[47] *Collected Works*, Vol. 55, p. 429. There were many who could not, for a variety of reasons, go to jail, and took to constructive work. Nirmala Shroff, widowed at a young age, took up khadi work in the 1930s and even today runs the khadi bhandar at Nana Chowk, Bombay. Interview, Bombay 9-6-1985. Maniben Nanavati, along with her 10-year old daughter, used to sell khadi in Vile Parle from door to door and travels to the Flora Fountain Khadi Bhandar everyday, at the age of 75. Interviews with Maniben Nanavati and her daughter, Aruna Purohit, Bombay, 28-5-1985. The well-known Communist leader, Ravi Narayan Reddy, went off to Kakinada as a student to take part in the Salt Satyagraha. His family came there, wept, and persuaded him to refrain from active participation in the movement and return to his village. He agreed on the condition that they finance a khadi-production centre, and he continued this work for one year. Interview, Hyderabad, 8-7-1984.

The hard core of constructive workers, especially the Ashramites, also provided a large number of cadre for the civil disobedience movements. Nearly all the leading constructive workers went to jail in the various *Satyagraha* struggles.[48] They were Gandhi's steel-frame. They were also the arteries through which the leadership kept in touch with the rural people. One of the secrets of Gandhi's uncanny political instinct was his contact with the people through the constructive workers with whom he maintained a continuous communication in person or through the mail.

Constructive workers were sturdy secularists and their work for Hindu-Muslim unity helped unify the people—a primary task by any reckoning. The work for the uplift of the Harijans and Adivasis, who formed the bulk of the agricultural labourers, was also very important, for there could be no united struggle against colonialism without their support, active or passive. They would otherwise also be open to attempts by colonial authorities to create divisions among the rural masses during periods of struggle. Khadi and Harijan work had another significance. Without their social and economic uplift, people who were suppressed for centuries were not able to conceive of participating in struggles of any kind. Contrary to certain present-day myths, the very poor and the demoralized do not find it easy to fight.[49] Constructive work filled these sections with a new hope, helped and trained them to lose their fear, made them self-reliant and enabled at least some of them to join the

[48]The life-histories of a large number of the freedom fighters whom we interviewed follow this pattern. For example, interview with Anavathukkal Achuthan, Kasargod, Kerala, 13-5-1984.

[49]We discovered in the course of our interviews that a major reason why Harijans did not participate to a significant extent in the national movement was their utter economic and social deprivation and cultural backwardness. This was also one reason why in most parts of the country they did not move into the politics of the left—both before and after independence—that is till the end of the 1960s. For example, interviews with K. Subramaniam 'Subri,' Madras, 7-6-1985; and Mallela Krupanandam, a Harijan participant, Nidubrolu, Guntur, A.P., 22-6-1984.

struggle for freedom and for their own social and economic advancement.[50]

VII

The complexity of the Congress strategy and the subtle manner in which it evolved and operated is brought out by the manner in which the Congress learnt to tackle constitutional work and constitutional reforms which formed a basic element of the equally complex colonial strategy and the semi-hegemonic character of the colonial state in India. The study of the interplay between the colonial and Congress strategies can serve as a fine example of how a hegemonic struggle is fought, but we can do so only briefly here.

Since the state was the terrain of struggle between the national movement and the colonial authorities, constitutional structures and constitutional reforms were not merely instruments and aspects of the colonial strategy of domination, they were simultaneously the fruits of the anti-colonial struggle, the ground that colonialism was forced to yield under nationalist pressure, a measure of the continually changing balance of forces. They represented, simultaneously, instruments of co-option by colonialism and widening of the democratic space in which the national movement could operate. The colonial rulers were forced to make constitutional concessions because of the very semi-hegemonic character of the state. They could not follow the logic of total suppression; suppression could only be a partial and short-term tactic. They had to develop non-suppressive forms to meet the nationalist challenge and to try and weaken the nationalist movement in the long run. They had to do so or give up the semi-hegemonic character of their rule and abandon the terrain of hegemonic struggle. They had to constantly legitimize their rule

[50]This was emphasized by the Harijan and low-caste participants whom we interviewed; for example, Mallela Krupanandam, Nidubrolu, Guntur, A.P., 22-6-1984, Appikatla Joseph, Vijayawada, 29-6-1984, Konada Suryaprakash Rao, Vijayawada, 26-6-1984 and Anavathukkal Achuthan, Kasargod, Malabar, 13-5-1984.

in the eyes of the ruled and public opinion at home or begin to openly live by the sword.

Long-term weakening of the national movement and strengthening of the British position in relation to it was to be secured by dividing the Congress internally and co-opting or integrating into the colonial constitutional and administrative structure its major segments. Each phase of suppression was therefore followed by a phase of constitutional reforms.[51] The reforms were invariably designed to achieve two major objectives: to convince large sections of Congressmen of the lack of need for extra-legal means and the efficacy of constitutionalism, of working from within the colonial structure. It was also hoped that Congressmen who had tasted parliamentary privileges and patronage (and later office) would be most reluctant to go back to mass politics or the politics of sacrifice. Reforms could also be used to promote dissensions and a split within the demoralized Congress ranks on the basis of constitutionalist vs. non-constitutionalist and right vs. left. The constitutionalists and the right-wing were to be placated through constitutional and other concessions, lured into the parliamentary game, encouraged to coalesce with the moderate liberals and landlords and other loyalists in working the reformed constitution, and enabled to increase their weight in the nationalist ranks.[52] The Extremists, the Gandhians and the left, it was hoped, would see all this as a compromise with

[51]That the intention of the reforms was not, as liberal imperialist historians would have it, to advance India towards independence or transfer of parts of state power was made clear by Lord Linlithgow, Chairman of Joint Parliamentary Committee on the Act of 1935, when he stated later that the Act had been framed "because we thought that was the best way ... of maintaining British influence in India. It is no part of our policy, I take it, to expedite in India constitutional changes for their own sake, or gratuitously to hurry the handing over of the controls to Indian hands at any pace faster than that which we regard as best calculated, on a long view, to hold India to the Empire." Quoted in R.J. Moore "The Problem of Freedom with Unity: London's India Policy, 1917-47," in D.A. Low, ed., *Congress and the Raj*, p. 379.

[52]"The only ultimate refuge lies in a split in the Congress, with the right joining moderate opinion outside in defence of the rights of property." Linlithgow to Haig, 23 October, 1938, *Haig Papers*, Roll 1, NMML.

imperialism and as abandonment of mass politics and would break away from the Congress or would be kicked out of it. Either way, the Congress would be split and weakened. Moreover, isolated from the constitutionalists and the right-wing, the extremist or radical elements could be smashed through police measures.[53] It was also for this reason that the colonial authorities refrained from taking strong action against revolutionary agitation by left-wing Congressmen from 1935 onwards.[54] In the 1930s, it was further hoped that Provincial Autonomy would create powerful provincial leaders in the Congress, who would become autonomous centres of political power, thus provincialising the Congress and eroding if not destroying the authority of its central all-India leadership.[55] Furthermore, Dyarchy in the 1920s and Provincial Autonomy in 1935 were expected to lead to a diversion of people's minds to provincial and local issues; making them forget, or at least not concentrate upon, the central or primary contradiction.

The Congress response was equally complex and in the end based on the dual character of the reforms. As is well known, this response was not readily formed; it evolved over the years through conflict and debate. Gandhi was firmly opposed to Council entry in the

[53]Linlithgow wrote to Zetland, the Secretary of State, on 5 March 1937: "It would, indeed, be convenient if the various sections in the Congress ranks were to part company and sort themselves out before action became necessary against the real revolutionaries." *Linlithgow Papers,* F. 125/4, NMML.

[54]Officials believed that Nehru and his followers had gone so far in their radicalism and in opposition to working the constitutional reforms of 1935 that they would not retreat but would rather split when defeated by the right wing in the AICC and at the Lucknow Congress. It was for this reason that nearly all the senior officials advised the Viceroy during 1935-36 not to arrest Nehru. Erskine, the Governor of Madras, for example, advised: "the more speeches of this type that Nehru makes the better, as his attitude will undoubtedly cause the Congress to split. Indeed, we should keep him in cotton wool and pamper him, for he is unwittingly smashing the Congress organization from inside." Erskine to Craik, April 20, 1936, *Home Political Proceedings,* F. No. 4/6/36.

[55]As Linlithgow wrote in 1936, "our best hope of avoiding a direct clash is in the potency of Provincial Autonomy to destroy the effectiveness of Congress as an All-India instrument of revolution." In John Glendevon, *The Viceroy at Bay,* p. 52.

1920s.[56] His opposition was diluted in the 1930s, but he became a supporter of parliamentary work only during 1937-38. Nehru led the opponents of office acceptance from 1935 to 1937, though he was converted during 1937.[57]

The nationalists had to follow the logic of the reforms as well as the logic of their own strategy. Once a space or terrain opened up for hegemonic struggle it had to be occupied. It could not be given up, it had to be used though in a creative, uncharted way. The reforms had to be worked; the question was in what manner. Basically, the answer was to work the reforms, not in the way the colonial authorities wanted, but by evolving and following an alternative method that would upset imperialist calculations and advance the nationalist cause.[58] The logic of the Congress position, which came to be accepted with near unanimity later though not during 1935-36, was put forward with disarming simplicity by Rajendra Prasad in a letter to Nehru in December 1935:[59]

[56]"He wrote in 1926: "I cannot reconcile myself to Council-entry. As time passes I feel more and more convinced that some of our troubles are due to the Council-entry." *Collected Works*, Vol. 30, p. 395.

[57]"My personal view was against office acceptance and so with your permission I want to give my views on the new experiment after it has been worked for the last few months. In my opinion, office acceptance has benefited us. The country is pulsating with a new life and new vision. As Congress President I go about in different parts of the country, and as such have ample opportunities of seeing and feeling how the kisans, peasants, labourers and traders are feeling as a result of the new experiment. Wherever Congress governments have been established, people are heaving a sigh of relief." Speech at the AICC Session in Calcutta, 29 October 1937, S. Gopal, ed., *Selected Works*, Vol. 8, p. 338. He reiterated this in a speech at Allahabad on 5 November 1937. "The greatest effect of office acceptance is the remarkable change it has brought about in the psychology of the people and the atmosphere in the country. There are certain things which cannot be weighed accurately in any scale. They are courage, sorrow and such feelings. One great advantage has been that the burden of the common people has been lightened to some extent. Some relief has been extended to the peasants and labourers. It was a great consideration that weighed in favour of office acceptance." *Ibid.*, pp. 350-1.

[58]See, for example, Gandhi in August 1938: "The Congress has entered upon office not to work the Act in the manner expected by the framers but in a manner so as to hasten the day of substituting it by a genuine Act of India's own coining." *Collected Works*, Vol. 67, p. 226.

[59]Rajendra Prasad to Nehru, 19 December 1935, in Jawaharlal Nehru, *A Bunch of Old Letters*, pp. 156-7.

> So far as I can judge no one wants to accept offices for their own sake. No one wants to work the constitution as the Government would like it to be worked. The questions for us are altogether different. What are we to do with this constitution? Are we to ignore it altogether and go our way? Is it possible to do so? Are we to capture it and use it as we would like to use it and to the extent it lends itself to be used in that way.... It is not a question to be answered *a priori* on the basis of pre-conceived notions of a so-called prochanger or nochanger, cooperator or obstructionist.
>
> I do not believe that any one has gone back to pre-non-cooperation mentality. I do not think we have gone back to 1923-28. We are in 1928-29 mentality and I have no doubt that better days will soon come.

The danger of co-option was clearly perceived both in the 1920s and the 1930s, but was not seen as inevitable. Work in the councils, including office-acceptance later, could also be used to defeat the colonial strategy and undermine colonial hegemony. As a Congressman put it in 1936: "Do not look upon ministries as offices, but as centres and fortresses from which British imperialism is radiated.... The Councils cannot lead us to constitutionalism for we are not babies; we will lead the Councils and use them for Revolution."[60] In fact, beginning with the 1880s, most Congressmen looked upon Councils and offices in the wider perspective of building and extending nationalist hegemony.

Nor should, it was held, such a vantage position be abandoned. In each case, in 1892, 1909, 1919, 1934, 1937, the colonial government was determined to hold elections and implement the reforms. This would certainly enable the Government to acquire some legitimacy. Moreover, even if the Congress did not work the reforms, there were other groups and parties, mostly pro-Government, who

[60] A.M. and S.G. Zaidi, editors, *The Encyclopaedia of the Indian National Congress,* Vol. 11, pp. 41-2.

were willing to do so. If the Congress left the field clear to them, they would use the legislatures—and later ministries—to weaken nationalism and encourage reactionary and communal policies and politics.

Lastly, despite their limited powers, the provincial legislatures and later ministries, which were after all also the result of the nationalists' own past efforts, could be and were used to promote constructive work, force the colonial state to promote economic development and provide some relief to the hard-pressed people.[61]

Work in the councils, municipal bodies and later ministries could also be used to build up self-confidence among the people and acquire prestige for the Congress and the national movement. For people who had been for long deprived of political power—and in the case of the majority all types of power—and subjected to the colonial ideology that they were incapable of exercising political power and that the colonial rulers could never be challenged, the strong speeches of a Pherozeshah Mehta or G.K. Gokhale, the defeats of the Government in the legislative assemblies during the 1920s and the wielding of elements of state power in the 1930s by the Congress, combined with the nationalists' exercising municipal power, would have provided a boost to their sense of self-worth and self-confidence.[62] The Congress Ministries greatly extended civil liberties in their provinces, and the result was a bourgeoning forth of the peasant, trade union and student movements.[63]

[61]Some of our interviewees who stressed this aspect of the work of the Congress Ministries were C. Subramaniam, Madras, 2-6-1984, Morarji Desai, Bombay, 14-6-1985, M. Bhaktavatsalam, Madras, 4-6-1984, Nageshwar Rao, Kavali, A.P., 17-6-1984, E.P. Gopalan, Koppam, Patambi, Palghat, Kerala, 18-5-1984, N. Krishnan Nair, Calicut, Kerala, 12-5-1984, A.V. Srikantha Poduval, Annur (Taliparamba), Kerala, 15-5-1984. It was for this reason, and because the possibilities of co-option were marginal, that Gandhians and radicals had no hesitation in taking up work in the municipal bodies.

[62]The same result was achieved in a massive fashion when the Government signed a pact with Gandhi in 1931 on an equal footing.

[63]Many left-wing activists emphasized this aspect of the Congress Ministries. Interviews with K. Murugesan, a Communist trade union leader, Madras, 9-6-1984, Achutha

The Congress calculations and counter strategy registered considerable success. Work in the councils did fill in the political void at a time when the national movement was recouping its strength. And those working in them did, on the whole, with some exceptions, avoid getting co-opted by the colonial state—and those who got co-opted soon lost their political standing in the Congress and in the country. The loss of a few was a small price to pay for the successful thwarting of colonial designs. The Swarajists in the 1920s and the Congress Ministries in 1939 demonstrated the success of the Congress approach and integrity by resigning their positions whenever asked to do so. The overwhelming majority worked in the legislatures and the ministries in a disciplined manner. Above all, from Pherozeshah Mehta and Gokhale to Motilal Nehru and the Congress Ministers and legislators of 1937-39, showed that it was possible to use legislatures and offices in a creative manner for promoting the politics of self-reliant anti-imperialism. They also successfully exposed the hollowness of colonial reforms and showed the people that India was still being essentially ruled from Britain in Britain's interests and with the aid of 'lawless laws' whenever the rulers found it in their interests to do so.

The Congress also avoided a split. Gandhi and the Gandhians in the 1920s and the left during 1936-39 refused to fall into the trap the colonial rulers had set for them. 'Provincialization' of the Congress also did not occur; throughout 1937-39 the Congress Ministries were guided and controlled by an all-India Congress Parliamentary Board and the Congress Working Committee on whose direction all of them resigned in 1939.

All this was possible because there was no real constitutionalist current inside the National Congress after 1920. Gandhi and Nehru were of course firmly committed to the view that *Satyagraha* alone

Menon, CPI leader, Trichur, 21-5-1984, V. Prasada Rao, a Communist leader of Andhra, New Delhi, 17-3-1985, M. Kumaran, a Communist leader. Badagara, Calicut, Kerala, 11-5-1984, Also see Visalakshi Menon, *National Movement, Congress Ministries and Imperial Policy: UP 1937-1939,* M. Phil dissertation.

could lead to freedom.[64] But basically this was true of nearly all Congressmen, including those in favour of council-entry in the 1920s and office-acceptance in the 1930s, who firmly believed that constitutional work was a short-term tactical step which the national movement had to take in view of its incapacity at that moment to resume the extra-legal mass movement. But they accepted that the 'real work lies outside the legislatures' and that, for achievement of freedom, the path of mass struggle outside the legal and constitutional framework was essential.[65] In both of its constitutional phases, all Congressmen agreed that it was necessary to coordinate work in the legislatures and ministries with mass politics—and they did in practice co-ordinate the two.[66] Nor did constitutional work or constitutionalists stand in the way of the rise of mass movements when the time became ripe for them—in 1928-29, in 1930, and again during World War II.

Above all, the Congress strategy regarding constitutional work was part not of a reformist framework but of a revolutionary framework. It was directed not at the gradual reform of colonial institutions and structures which would lead to freedom, but aimed at the replacement of the colonial state, though the replacement would occur through transfer of power and not through its seizure.[67] Legislatures were seen not as arenas for the transformation of the colonial state but of struggle against it. This was another reason why it was found impossible to co-opt the Congress or the Congress-led national movement. Herein lay, we may point out as an aside, a

[64]Gandhi said in 1934 when giving support to those who wanted to fight elections to the Central Legislative Assembly: "I hope that the majority will always remain untouched by the glamour of council work. In its own place, it will be useful. But the Congress will commit suicide if its attention is solely devoted to legislative work. Swaraj will never come that way. Swaraj can only come through an all-round consciousness of the masses." *Collected Works,* Vol. 58, p. 11.

[65]In Y.S. Chavan's words, "constitutional struggle was another form of struggle though the *real* basis was mass struggle." Interview, New Delhi, 2-5-1984.

[66]Visalakshi Menon, *op. cit.*

[67]See "Elements of Continuity and Change in the Early Nationalist Activity," in Bipan Chandra, *Nationalism and Colonialism in Modern India.*

crucial difference between Gandhi and his contemporaries, the European Social Democrats. Gandhi used the language of reform and *compromise* but he stood for anti-colonial revolution; the Social Democrats used the language of revolution but were wholly co-opted by the capitalist state.

VIII

Non-violence was a multi-hued concept and phenomenon. We will here deal only with those of its aspects which relate to the over-all strategy of the national movement, for it was an essential component of this strategy as a form of political action and behaviour. In fact, non- violence had informed the strategy of the Congress from its very inception. It was not a mere dogma of an individual[68] or a clever use of the propertied classes, it was in some essential ways integral to the nature of the Indian national movement as a hegemonic movement based on wide mass mobilization. At the same time, the point of *differentia specifica* of the national movement was not its non-violent form of struggle, but its hegemonic and mass character. Because of this character, non-violence became one of its basic elements.

The adoption of non-violent forms of struggle enabled the participation of the mass of the people who could not have participated in a similar manner, or whose involvement could not have been so deep, in a movement that adopted violent forms. The 'costs' of participating in a violent movement are necessarily much higher, in terms of repression and otherwise, and relatively fewer numbers tend to join. Participation in violent activity, whether of a terrorist or a guerilla nature, or in an army of liberation, necessarily involves long absences from home, total disruption of normal life, complete abandonment of normal livelihood, and loss of life. Non-

[68]Gandhi several times clarified that while for him non-violence was a matter of principle, an article of faith, he asked the people and the national movement to accept it as a matter of policy and on grounds of practical necessity.

violent struggle, though it too involved jail-going and therefore disruption of normal activity, was qualitatively different in terms of cost. Moreover, it had enough room for participation without the extreme step of courting arrest. In any case, the knowledge that the degree of repression would be much less than in the case of resort to violent action encouraged many, especially from among the poorer sections, to join. Many of our interviewees emphasized the role of non-violence in enabling the mass of the people to participate in the movement.[69] We were also told by any number of women participants that non-violence facilitated their participation in the struggle; the resistance from families, fear of repression, etc., was much less than if they had wanted to join a violent movement. In any case, women would, they said, find it difficult to join armed struggle in large numbers. But, they said, when it came to undergoing suffering, facing lathi-charges, etc., women were probably stronger than men.[70]

Non-violence as a form of struggle and political behaviour was also of course linked to the semi-hegemonic character of the colonial state and the democratic character of British polity. Non-violence also included within it civil behaviour toward the 'enemy,' that is the colonial bureaucracy in India. It meant making an appeal to the 'finer instincts' of the adversary; it meant above all fighting on the terrain of moral force. But then, as we have already seen, the terrain of hegemonic struggle is also that of moral force.

Non-violent mass movements placed the adversary morally in the wrong and exposed the coercive base or underpinning of state power, when the authorities used armed force against peaceful

[69]For example, interviews with C. Subramaniam, Madras, 2-6-1984, D.K. Kunte, *op. cit.,* P.K. Kunte, Bombay, 24-5-1985, Madhavlal Shankarlal Pandya, *op. cit.,* Lalbhai Dahyabhai Naik, *op. cit.,* Vaid Pashabhai Bhailalbhai Amin, Anand, Gujarat, 4-7-1985, Tribhuvandas Patel, Anand, Gujarat, 1-7-1985.

[70]For example, interviews with A.V. Kuttimalu Ararai, Ernakulam, 23-5-1984, Mrinalini Desai, Bombay, 22-5-1985, Tummala Durgamma, Guntur, A.P., 23-6-1984, Kalluri Tulsiamma, Guntur, A.P., 23-6-1984. Gandhi too noted that "satyagraha is a struggle in which the oldest and the weakest in body may take part, if they have stout hearts." *Collected Works,* Vol. 68, p. 387.

Satyagrahis. In fact, a non-violent mass movement put the rulers on the horns of a dilemma.[71] If they hesitated to suppress it because it was peaceful, they lost an important part of their hegemony, because the civil resisters did break existing laws and not to take action against them amounted to abdication of administrative authority and a confession of incapacity or lack of strength to rule. The foundations of foreign rule which rested on a small number of foreigners in the bureaucracy, police and army and on a small number of loyalist Indians were seriously undermined. If they suppressed the movement, they still lost, for it was morally difficult to justify the suppression of a peaceful movement and non-violent law-breakers through the use of force. They were in a damned if you do, damned if you don't situation. The national movement had, on the other hand, a winning strategy: a semi-democratic rule had really no answer to a mass movement that was non-violent and had massive popular support. In practice, the colonial authorities constantly vacillated between the two choices, usually plumping in the end in favour of suppression. By taking recourse to suppression of a peaceful movement they had to suffer constant erosion of hegemony by exposing the basic under-pinnings in force and coercion of colonial rule.[72] Furthermore, unlike in a democratic and hegemonic society the colonial state could not fight a popular opposition on the political and ideological terrain, and on its own

[71]See Sucheta Mahajan, *op. cit.*

[72]The sight of policemen beating up peaceful civil resisters was often the signal for many bystanders to jump into the fray. An interviewee told us how the sight of a little girl holding the national flag aloft and marching bravely towards an armed posse of policemen, in the heady days of August 1942, affected her. She ran from her house and took the flag from the little girl to prevent her being beaten up by the police. A scuffle ensued, and she landed up in jail, but was released soon thereafter. However, she now graduated from a sympathetic onlooker to an active mobiliser, organized a procession in defiance of the D.I.R., went back to jail and was now convicted. Afterwards, she devoted her entire life to constructive work among Harijans in a remote Gujarat village. Sarla Devi Mazumdar, Interview, Bombay, 29-5-1985. There were many by-standers who, for a variety of reasons, could not court arrest or join the resisters. They rushed to the nearest khadi bhandar, tore off their foreign clothes, stamped on them, and donned khadi.

terrain—the terrain of law and order—the colonial state invariably lost. Its hegemony or its moral basis were destroyed bit by bit.[73]

Adoption of non-violence by the national movement was also linked to the fact that a disarmed people had hardly any other recourse. On the one hand, the colonial state had through an elaborate system completely disarmed the Indian people since 1858 and made it difficult for them to obtain arms or training in their use; on the other hand, it was a strong and not an inert state.[74] The leaders of the national movement understood from the beginning that Indians did not possess the material resources necessary to wage war against such a strong state. In non-violent struggle, on the other hand, it is moral strength and mass support that count and here a disarmed people are not at a disadvantage.[75] In other words, non-violence is also a way of becoming equal in political resources to an armed state in a war of position. Basic here was the understanding that the disarmed Indian people would not be able to withstand massive government repression, that they were not yet trained to do so, and that use of violence would provide justification to the Government for launching a massive attack on the popular movement.[76] Such heavy repression would demoralize the people and lead to political passivity.[77] Non-violence thus not only reduced

[73]The obverse is also, of course, true. In a hegemonic struggle, what appears to be an unprovoked recourse to violence on the part of the movement also leads to the erosion of its popular support and moral strength.

[74]Many contemporaries, as also many later writers, made the mistake of seeing the marked tendency of the colonial regime to rely on legal and administrative rules and procedure as inertness, In fact, no state remains inert in face of danger; the question always is whether it has the will and the capacity to act, when necessary, in a hard manner. The colonial state in India had both.

[75]Both these perceptions were widely held by nearly all our non-Communist and some of the Communist interviewees

[76]In this aspect, non-violence meant not giving the Government a moral opportunity to strike hard at the movement. This, of course, assumes that either the Government would not strike without being provided such an opportunity, or, if it did, it would pay a very heavy price in terms of loss of hegemony.

[77]Several interviewees told us that their experience was that when the police crushed a violent upsurge it demoralized the people but when it attacked non-violent picketers or *Satyagrahis*, the people felt angry and wanted to express their solidarity with the freedom movement in some form or capacity.

the cost of political struggle, bringing it within the capacity of the mass of people to bear, but it also shamed the rulers into good behaviour and forced them to operate in terms of the 'better part of their nature.' As pointed out earlier, non-violent protest and civil behaviour towards the bureaucracy tended to under-mine its morale and neutralize it in political terms, and even win over some of its individual members. A retired British ICS, Thomas Gay, told us that nothing destroyed the morale of the public-school educated British civil servant more than having to lathi-charge unarmed men and women who could not or would not hit back at you at all.[78] It is difficult to resist the temptation to quote a long extract from H.V.R. Iyengar's oral testimony where he describes a scene in Bombay in 1931. He was atop the terrace of Victoria Terminus along with Sir Ernest Hotson, Home Member, Bombay, watching an enormous crowd trying to take out a procession in defiance of prohibitory orders, and the police trying to stop them:[79]

> There used to be British sergeants in the police forces in those days and they mercilessly beat them up. Several people were seriously injured, but the procession did not stop. You cannot go on beating people who offer no resistance. The result of this non-violent resistance was that there were thousands and thousands of people in the city of Bombay—I think the figure for the whole of India was a couple of lakhs of people—who were put in jail. There was a limit beyond which they found it difficult to use force. Now if a procession is coming and the procession becomes rowdy and also gets violent, then your blood is up; you want to

[78]Thomas Gay, Interview, Pune, 9-6-1985. A taluka level leader, D.K. Kunte told us that "by our non-violence we told the tehsildars and other lower level officials that we are not your enemies." *Op. cit.* Umashankar Joshi stressed the same point. Interview, Ahmedabad, 7-7-1985.

[79]*Oral history transcript,* NMML. Iyengar was then a young I.C.S. Officer in the Bombay Secretariat; he was the Home Secretary in Bombay in 1942, Home Secretary, Government of India, in 1948, Principal Private Secretary to Nehru subsequently and Governor of the Reserve Bank of India from 1957.

> give tit for tat, you have no hesitation in firing at such a crowd. But if you fire at a completely unarmed crowd and fellows try to march ahead with their arms folded, then the police can beat them up; they can even draw blood; but if the other fellow does not resist, takes his punishment, you can not go on beating up the person.... There were hefty Sikhs, Pathans and other able-bodied Hindus, they were marching in front of the procession, they were beaten up—and some of them were beaten up badly—but they did not retaliate, as a result of which the sergeants started scratching their heads—that was a situation to which they had not been accustomed. The result was that they just stopped beating them up, and Sir Ernest Hotson did not know what to do because these people went on folding their hands and the police, after sometime, stopped beating them. That was the situation. This was part and parcel of the whole campaign. It was an unusual campaign in world's history and something to which the British had certainly not been accustomed. If somebody had thrown stones against the police, I expect that they would have opened out the guns to shoot the people. I remember from personal knowledge, a number of my English colleagues in the civil service were fundamentally decent, kindly lot of men, and although they did not like certain things, and probably hated the Congress movement and wanted to run the thing down, they just did not feel that they should go beyond a particular point in trying to resist this movement.

Our discussion so far leads to two larger questions. Can a mass movement be violent, or, as suggested by Jawaharlal Nehru and Bhagat Singh in short but pregnant statements, do mass movements in which millions participate—as distinguished from cadre based movements—have to be, by their very nature, non-violent.[80]

[80]"Use of force justifiable when resorted to as a matter of terrible necessity: non-violence as a policy indispensable for all mass movements." Bhagat Singh, *Why I am an Atheist* (with an Introduction by Bipan Chandra), pamphlet, Shaheed Bhagat Singh Research Committee, Delhi, 1979. "Any great movement for liberation today must necessarily be a

Secondly, non-violence in a movement need not *per se* be seen as non-revolutionary, for it may be an essential part of a revolutionary strategy of hegemonic struggle—a war of position—for the change in the structure of state and society. This is particularly so if "the revolutionary nature of any particular movement flows not from its forms of struggle, or methods of mobilization, but from the nature of the primary contradiction that is sought to be resolved, its social and political objectives, its ability to mobilize and politicize wide sections of the masses, its capacity to challenge the existing order and pose the question of structural change, its long-term impact on areas and social classes not directly involved in the struggle, on society as a whole, and on the relationships of power and exploitation."[81]

Once the basic character and objectives of the Congress strategy are grasped, once it is realized that both phases of the national movement, war of manoeuvre and war of position, are geared to the twin tasks of winning the hearts and minds of Indian people and making them active participants in the movement and makers of their own history, the success and failure of the Congress-led movement as a whole and of its extra-legal mass movements in particular have to be evaluated in a new manner. The concepts of success and defeat in a hegemonic struggle are very different from those in an armed struggle. The criterion of success or failure here is the extent to which colonial hegemony over the Indian people and its own bureaucracy is under-mined and the people are politicized, prepared for struggle and their capacity to fight enhanced. Judged in this light, we would see that these objectives were progressively

mass movement, and mass movements must essentially be peaceful, except in times of organized revolt. Whether we have the non-cooperation of a decade ago or the modern industrial weapon of the general strike, the basis is peaceful organization and peaceful action." *Selected Works of Jawaharlal Nehru,* Vol. 4, p. 195. Of course, where the state does not provide space for mass movements, movements for the overthrow of the state and for social transformation have no choice but to operate on the terrain of armed struggle.

[81]Mridula Mukherjee, "Peasant Resistance and Peasant Consciousness in Colonial India: A Historiographical Critique."

achieved through successive waves of mass movements alternating with phases of truce even when the mass movements were suppressed (1932, 1942), withdrawn (1922), ignored (1940-41), or ended in a compromise (1930-31, but the Round Table Conference failed) and were therefore apparently defeated in terms of their stated objective of winning freedom. In terms of hegemony, these movements were great successes and marked leaps in mass political consciousness.[82] The movements were successfully crushed, for the people were cowed down, if only for the time being, by superior force. But their faith in the Congress had leaped forward; they had been further transformed; their will to fight had been further strengthened; their faith in British rule and its invincibility further eroded. Symbolic of the real outcome, of the real impact of civil disobedience was the heroes' welcome given to prisoners on their release in 1934 and again later in 1945. As H.N. Brailsford, the Labourite journalist, wrote assessing the results of the 1930 struggle: the Indians "had freed their own minds, they had won independence in their hearts.... A lasting change had happened in the minds of the hundreds of thousands who went to prison and millions who faced the lathis of the police. It was enough to perform even a symbolic act of rebellion by making salt, or to picket a cloth shop as thousands of shy and sheltered women did. By these acts they broke the paralysis, the consciousness of a predestined inferiority."[83]

That this was not obvious to all the contemporaries is clear from the twin comments of Willingdon, the Viceroy, who declared in early 1933: "The Congress is in a definitely less favourable position than in 1930, and has lost its hold on the public."[84] And then bewailed in 1934 when the elections to the Central Legislative Assembly produced a triumph for the Congress: "Singularly

[82]"We didn't win in any of the movements and yet in 1947 the British vacated." Morarji Desai, Interview, Bombay, 14-6-1985.

[83]Quoted in Bisheshwar Prasad, *Bondage and Freedom,* Vol. II, p. 423.

[84]Quoted in B.R. Nanda, *Mahatma Gandhi, A Biography,* p. 339.

unfortunate a great triumph for little Gandhi."[85] He did not make the connection between the apparent suppression and defeat of the 1932-34 movement and its real success in terms of spread of hegemony. He was utterly unaware that the 'great triumph for little Gandhi' was related to the strategy of the struggle; the strategy was precisely designed to achieve this result. This is what hegemonic struggle is all about.

On the other hand, Gandhi was quite conscious of the real efficacy, the true nature and outcome of the 'defeated' movements in terms of hegemony. Applying balm to Nehru's despondent heart, he wrote in September 1933: "I have no sense of defeat in me and the hope in me that this country of ours is fast marching towards its goal, is burning as bright as it did in 1920."[86]

[85]Quoted in D.A. Low, "'Civil Martial Law': The Government of India and the Civil Disobedience Movements, 1930-34," in D.A. Low, ed., *Congress and the Raj*, p. 190.

[86]*Collected Works*, Vol. 55, p. 430. The Congress Working Committee too showed awareness of the hegemonic aspect of mass movements in its statement withdrawing the Civil Disobedience Movement: "Without non-violent non-cooperation and civil resistance there would never have been the phenomenal mass awakening that has taken place throughout the country." *Tendulkar, op. cit.* Vol. 3, p. 302.

CHAPTER 4

Masses and Leaders

One of the most important and complex problems faced by a mass movement, as also its historians, is to establish a correct relation between the roles of masses and leaders, between spontaneity and organization (and guidance from the top), between popular consciousness and its transformation. It is not possible to study the national movement either by concentrating on the activity of the leaders as many traditional nationalist historians have done or by drawing a dividing line between the masses and their leaders and seeing them as antagonists as some have been advocating in recent years.

A movement by definition must have a leadership, but it becomes a mass movement only when people join it. A mass movement has to be based on the urges of the masses and on popular consciousness. The leadership cannot create a movement at will and then stimulate and persuade the masses to join in. Propelled by both objective and subjective forces, the masses move in the direction of a movement on their own. At the same time, leadership or headquarters or a centre is essential in any mass movement. There can be no movement without it. In other words, a mass movement involves, or is, a dialectical process in which the consciousness and the spontaneous self-activity of the masses are integrated with the ideological, organizational and political direction of the leadership; there has to be a 'unity between spontaneity and conscious direction.' Leadership can neither be imposed on the masses from the top, nor can the masses in political motion do without a leadership which is integrated with them. The success or failure or rather the very coming into being of a mass movement depends on a correct evolution of this process.

Similarly, political work in a mass movement has to be based on the people's consciousness, on their lived experience, on their spontaneously or 'autonomously' arising discontent and disillusionment and perception of oppression and suppression and need for change, and on their capacity to struggle and sacrifice. But leaders have not only to respond to the people, not only to reflect mass consciousness, they have also to further politically arouse, educate and guide it. Despite their anger or discontent the masses lack the intellectual tools or the capacity to comprehend the broader social reality or the sources of their discontent which would enable them to act on the basis of their discontent or to formulate meaningful alternatives to their social condition.[1] They may not, on their own, even perceive fully or adequately their own interests. Leadership is needed to grasp and spread a complex understanding of complex forces. Similarly, leaders need to have faith in the capacity of the masses to struggle; at the same time, they have to undertake the task of educating the masses into this faith in themselves and of further developing this capacity.

Once the leaders and the masses are united on basic goals, objectives and values, leadership is also necessary to articulate popular demands and aspirations, to forge a right type of and effective organization for politics and mass struggle, to prepare people ideologically and politically for struggles, to mobilize an atomized and dispersed people (this is especially so in an agrarian society), to generate popular politics on a nation-wide scale, to

[1]Cf. Gramsci: "Critical self-consciousness means, historically and politically, the creation of an *elite* of intellectuals. A human mass does not 'distinguish' itself, does not become independent in its own right without, in the widest sense, organizing itself; and there is no organization without intellectuals, that is without organizers and leaders." *Selections from the Prison Notebooks,* p. 334. Narrating his experiences of the Tebhaga peasant struggle, Sunil Sen told us that spontaneous consciousness has to be there for struggle on an immediate demand or against an act or measure of felt injustice but that to take the struggle to higher stages there has to be a conscious guidance from above.

create the very nation or people who would struggle together, and to evolve correct strategy and tactics which would correspond to the specific historical situation. In the absence of any of these necessary 'services' which a leadership provides, no sustained popular struggle capable of bringing about basic transformation of social conditions may ensue despite the existence of social contradictions, spontaneous discontent or the basic desire to change the social condition. Or a spontaneous and sporadic struggle may occur which is, despite immense heroism and sacrifice, doomed to ineffectivity and defeat from the beginning. Or, alternatively, a struggle may not occur or assume viable proportions if the leadership fails to perceive the reality correctly or perform its other functions in a historically adequate manner.[2]

In reality, masses vs. leadership and spontaneity vs. organization are false dichotomies. The question, in fact, is that of the manner in which in real life leaders and masses or followers relate to each other in a mass movement. The question is whether a movement is able to have "a matching of thrusts from below with orders from above."[3] In Indian conditions, if the political activists assumed or the historian assumes today that the masses, who were the chief victims of colonialism, lacked awareness of their oppression or the desire to overthrow their social condition as well as the capacity to develop this awareness or desire, it would lead to passive, elitist politics or elitist view of the national movement, so fashionable in recent years, namely, that the upper classes or power-seeking politicians manipulated the people through nationalist ideology to serve their own ends. As pointed out earlier, these schools of historians following in the footsteps of their colonial predecessors would deny either the existence of the primary contradiction or the people's instinctive awareness of it on the basis of their daily experience as

[2]The failure of a large number of our contemporary radical parties and groups to convince the people, living in conditions of extreme poverty and misery and filled with great deal of discontent and social anger, to rise up in struggle under the aegis of these parties or groups or on their own is an indicator.

[3]Gramsci, *op. cit.*, p. 188.

well as their capacity to develop a fuller understanding of its mechanics.[4]

At the same time, to believe that the primary contradiction spontaneously, on its own, generates among the people a fully developed understanding of colonialism and the desire and capacity to overthrow it as a system or structure is to assume the existence of a consciousness which in reality had to be consciously and constantly aroused, educated and developed. This view also leads to the belief that the people are ever ready for struggle against colonial authorities and that those sections of the people who are most oppressed have the greatest capacity as well as consciousness to take part in, or lead, this struggle. In fact, both these views would deny the importance of the role and quality of leadership which had to have the capacity to perceive the inherent, instinctive, nascent anti-colonial consciousness of the masses and, at the same time, to understand the contrary elements, conditions, processes, constraints, which blocked the development of this consciousness and prevented purposeful political action.[5] In other words, a mature leadership had to base itself upon as well as transform popular anti-colonial consciousness.[6]

[4]It may also lead to another wrong understanding of anti-imperialist struggle. Since it is believed that the masses cannot have an anti-colonial or nationalist consciousness on their own, they can be brought into nationalist politics only by appealing to their class instincts, taking up their class demands and then showing that colonialism supports their class enemies. This view, while believing in the existence of class instincts, denies the possibility of the existence of national or anti-imperialist instincts. This view thus not only denies any spontaneously or autonomously developing national, anti-colonial consciousness to the masses, but inevitably leads to the blurring of the primary contradiction and, in practice, concentration on the inner-contridictions of colonial society.

[5]These can be the relations and conditions of domination themselves, incapacity to see the overall reality, lack of organizational capacity to wage a large-scale struggle in terms of both territory or space and numbers, absence of leadership itself, etc.

[6]Cf. Gramsci: "But innovation cannot come from the mass, at least at the beginning, except through the mediation of an *elite* for whom the conception implicit in human activity has already become to a certain degree a coherent and systematic ever-present awareness and a precise and decisive will." *Ibid.*, p. 335. Commenting on this passage, Joseph V. Femia says that for Gramsci "the party, then, is the necessary mediating force which enables the masses to transcend their mystified condition." *Gramsci's Political Thought,* p. 136.

In the Moderate phase, the nationalist leadership concentrated on the evolution of headquarters and that too primarily at the ideological plane. The masses were seen as socially backward and politically passive, though the Moderates hoped to educate them and gradually and in time bring them into active politics. They did, however, succeed in evolving a complex understanding of colonial exploitation and its impact on the Indian people. Lokamanya Tilak, Bipin Chandra Pal, Aurobindo Ghosh and other Extremist leaders recognized the basic role of the masses in the anti-imperialist struggle and had an immense faith in their capacity to wage this struggle. They therefore wanted to base their politics on the masses. But, in practice, they could neither reach out to them nor grasp the role and significance of the self activity of the masses. The masses were seen as inflammable raw material which the leadership had to ignite through intense agitational and other activity among the masses. It was in the Gandhian phase that a better understanding and practice of the dialectic between the masses and leaders or spontaneity and organization were evolved. It was above all Gandhi who by and large understood this dialectic, reached out to the masses, mobilized them on the basis of their own political activity, that is, recognized that a mass movement can arise and develop and move towards success only when the masses are the subjects and not objects of politics. Also, the Gandhian era leadership simultaneously based itself on the anti-colonial consciousness of the masses and further educated and developed it on the basis of the complex and scientific understanding of colonial exploitation developed by the Moderates.

Though Gandhi tried to solve the masses-leaders problem in his political practice from the South African days, it was in the 1930s and early 1940s that he thought about it in more explicit terms.

Gandhi had immense faith in the capacity of the masses to fight—in their fearlessness, courage, capacity to sacrifice and strength. He based his entire politics on their militancy and self-sacrificing spirit. Asking K.F. Nariman and others not to get demoralized by the petering out of the Civil Disobedience Movement, he said in

1934: "The nation has got energy of which you have no conception but I have." At the same time, he said, a leadership should not "put an undue strain on the energy."[7] It should also follow a strategy and tactics which enhance people's fearlessness[8] and "consciousness of their strength."[9] This understanding of the dialectic between popular consciousness and leadership emerged very clearly in his reply to Louis Fischer's question in June 1942 about how he hoped to organize a movement which would put an end to a mighty empire. He said: "I will appeal to the people's instincts. I may arouse them."[10] Earlier in February 1939, while commenting on the general repressive measures in the states, he had written in the *Harijan:* "If the people have shed fear and learnt the art of self-sacrifice, *they need no favours.* Kicks can never cow them. *They will take what they need and assimilate it.*"[11]

Gandhi well understood that a mass movement had to be based on the active participation of the people and that it could not be sustained only by the highly motivated cadre or 'the standing army.' It was with "the might of the dumb millions" that he planned "to resist the might of that Empire" in 1942.[12] That he was acutely aware that too great an exercise of his personal influence in securing concessions for a movement could lead to the political passivity of the people is evident from the explanation he gave for his withdrawal from the Gwyer Award on Rajkot in 1939, which had been prompted by his indefinite fast. He told the people of Rajkot: "Your energies would have been rusting, and your hands would have been crippled."[13] In other words, it was not winning a demand but

[7] *Collected Works,* Vol. 57, p. 454.
[8] *Ibid.,* Vol. 55, p. 429.
[9] *Ibid.,* Vol. 68, p. 319.
[10] *Ibid.,* Vol. 76, p. 450.
[11] *Ibid.,* Vol. 68, p. 357 (Emphasis added).
[12] *Ibid.,* Vol. 76, p. 397. When asked by a journalist whether the projected movement would not go to pieces if he and Nehru were arrested, Gandhi's answer was: "No, not if we have worked among the people." *Ibid.,* p. 193.
[13] *Ibid.,* Vol. 69, p. 274. Also see, *ibid.,* pp. 274-5.

how you won it that was important; crucial here was the participation and the political education of the people.

Gandhi never tired of pointing out that leaders could not create movements; it was the people who created them. The people had to move towards a movement on their own. Leaders could 'start' a movement and lead it only when they correctly gauged the people's mood. They could give it only that direction which was basically or intrinsically in keeping with the people's inclinations, desires or consciousness. Explaining the shift in Congress policy towards the states during 1938-39 from non-intervention to intervention, Gandhi wrote in the *Harijan* on 28 January 1939: "The policy of non-intervention by the Congress was, in my opinion, a perfect piece of statesmanship when the people of the States were not awakened. That policy would be cowardice when there is all-round awakening among the people of the States and a determination to go through a long course of suffering for the vindication of their just rights.... The moment they (the people) became ready, the legal, constitutional and artificial boundary was destroyed."[14] In a brilliant passage in the *Harijan* of 11 February 1939 he formulated his perception of the political relationship between leaders, mass awakening and a mass movement: "Yet the awakening of millions does take time. It cannot be manufactured. It comes or seems to come mysteriously. National workers can merely hasten the process by anticipating the mass mind."[15]

That a leadership could not manipulate the people any way they wanted and that people and their politics had an autonomy of their own to which the leaders had to relate in a positive manner was made clear by Gandhi during his discussion of the projected Quit India movement in 1942. Answering a question by Stuart Emeny of the

[14] *Ibid.*, Vol. 68, pp. 326-7.

[15] *Ibid.*, p. 381. Earlier, referring to efforts to superimpose ideas and concepts on the people—in this case the Roman script—he had said: "And all superimpositions will be swept out of existence when the true mass awakening comes, as it is coming, much sooner than anyone of us can expect from known causes." *Ibid.*

News Chronicle (London) whether the Congress leaders did not "have a moral duty to stand beside the Russians and the Chinese," he replied: "Don't you see if it was a purely personal question, what you say would have been perfectly possible. But even with the combined influence of every member of the Working Committee, it would have been impossible to enthuse the masses in favour of the Allied cause, which they do not understand, cannot understand." But surely, said Emeny, "You could, if you would, with your tremendous authority with the masses, do anything. They are sure to listen to you." Gandhi replied: "You credit me with an influence which I wish I had but, 1 assure you, I do not possess." After giving two examples of his failure to carry the people with him, he said: "my influence, great as it may appear to outsiders, is strictly limited. I may have considerable influence to conduct a campaign for redress of popular grievances *because people are ready and need a helper.* But I have no influence to direct people's energy in a channel in which they have no interest."[16]

In 1947, when asked by a colleague why he did not create a situation favourable to struggle, he said:[17]

> I have never created a situation in my life. I have one qualification which many of you do not possess. I can almost instinctively feel what is stirring in the heart of the masses. And when I feel that the forces of good are dimly stirring within, I seize upon them and build up a programme. And they respond. People say that I had created a situation; but I had done nothing except giving a shape to what was already there. Today I see no sign of

[16]*Ibid.*, Vol. 76, p. 300 (Emphasis added). As if to further emphasize this point, he said a little later: "The awakening that showed itself on 6 April 1919, was a matter of surprise to every Indian. 1 cannot today account for the response we then had from every nook and corner of the country where no public worker had ever been. We had not then gone among the masses, we did not know we could go and speak to them." *Ibid.*, p. 302.

[17]N.K. Bose, "My Experiences as a Gandhian-II," quoted in Bimal Prasad, *Gandhi, Nehru and J.P.*, p. 31.

such a healthy feeling. And therefore I shall have to wait until the time comes.

Two last quotations regarding the relation that leaders' political activity bears to the activity of the masses. During his controversy with Subhas Bose in 1939, Gandhi wrote to the latter: "My prestige does not count. It has no independent value of its own .... India will rise or fall by the quality of the sum total of the acts of her many millions. Individuals, however high they may be, are of no account except in so far as they represent the many millions."[18] Earlier, in 1915, referring to the common people who fought along with him in South Africa, in the course of his reply to an address of welcome at Madras, he said: "You have said that I inspired these great men and women, but I cannot accept that proposition. It was they, the simple-minded folk, who worked away in faith, never expecting the slightest reward, who inspired me, who kept me to the proper level, and who compelled me by their great sacrifice, by their great faith, by their great trust in the great God to do the work that 1 was able to do."[19]

At the same time, Gandhi asserted that leadership was essential to any mass movement.[20] The metaphor he often used was that of an army where the soldiers and the generals played essential but complementary roles. The Congress leadership too was clear on the need for a strong, continuous, and disciplined leadership and single-mindedness of command, despite the open and democratic character of the Indian national movement. Consequently, at the beginning of every mass struggle it reiterated the essentiality of Gandhi's leadership.[21]

[18] *Collected Works*, Vol. 69, p. 97.

[19] *Ibid.*, Vol. 13, pp. 52-3.

[20] See, for example, *ibid.*, Vol. 55, p. 428.

[21] See, for example, the 8 August 1942 Quit India Resolution of the AICC. Tendulkar, *op. cit.*, Vol. 6, p. 151.

While emphasizing the role of democratic functioning and free expression of views within the party and the movement[22] and the primary role of the masses in the struggle, Gandhi did not hesitate to stress the role of discipline. A mass movement, he repeatedly remarked, especially during 1939 when the country was getting ready for a struggle, was like waging a war and the *satyagrahi* was like a soldier of the non-violent army. He or she must observe army-like, cast-iron discipline. Ordinary people could become a political force only through discipline. This was even more so when they were engaged in a war—"a life and death struggle"—with a mighty enemy—British imperialism, "the most experienced and organized corporation in the world." The people had a right to change their leader if he no longer commanded their confidence. They, then, must appoint another leader in his place. But so long as they

[22]Thus, having drafted the Working Committee resolution for taking disciplinary action against Subhas Bose for defying the party leadership's efforts to reorganize the Bengal Provincial Congress Committee and thus violating party discipline and disobeying the orders of the Congress President without appealing to the Working Committee, AICC, etc., Gandhi defended Bose's "perfect right to agitate against the action of the Working Committee and canvass public opinion against it." He further said: "And those who disapprove of the action of the Working Committee are certainly entitled to join any demonstration in favour of Subhas Babu. Unless this simple rule is observed we shall never evolve democracy." Both sides to the dispute, pro-Working Committee and pro- Subhas groups, could express their viewpoints by holding meetings and counter meetings. "These meetings, both for and against, should be regarded as a means of educating public opinion." Referring to the use of disciplinary powers against those who broke discipline or opposed the leadership, he wrote: "If it is true, as it is true, that no organization can do without such powers, it is equally true that no organization that makes free use of such powers has any right to exist. It cannot. It has then obviously lost the public backing." *Collected Works,* Vol. 70, pp. 150-1. Similarly, in his famous 'Do or Die' speech on 8 August 1942, at the very beginning he congratulated the Communists who had pressed their amendments to a division and voted against the Quit India resolution. "In doing so," he said, "they had nothing to be ashamed of. For the last 20 years we have tried to learn not to lose courage even when we are in a hopeless minority and are laughed at. We have learned to hold on to our beliefs in the confidence that we are in the right. It behoves us to cultivate this courage of conviction, for it ennobles man and raises his moral stature. I was, therefore, glad to see that these friends had imbibed the principle which I have tried to follow for the last fifty years and more." *Ibid.,* Vol. 76, p. 384.

accepted a person as a leader, they must accept his command; a leader could not accept their dictation. A leader of the mass movement was like a physician or a general in battle and not like a popular representative of a group of people (and the leadership was like the army head-quarters). His command was to be obeyed; his orders had to be carried out.[23]

Elements of the basic strategy of the movement and the nature of the relation between leaders and followers and spontaneity and organization in it can be seen through the style and conduct of the mass movements of the Gandhian era.[24] Every struggle, being basically hegemonic, was carefully prepared politically and ideologically. The extent of the readiness of the people was carefully gauged—and here the role of the leadership's instinct was important.[25] Gandhi both actively prepared the people for struggle and patiently waited for their spirit to arise. The tempo of the movement was slowly and gradually built up to correspond to the rising tempo of the people, the threads of varied politics were gathered in the hands of the leadership, the public opinion was built up, the resources of hegemony over the Indian people, the British

[23]*Ibid* Vol. 67, pp. 225-6, 401; Vol. 69, pp. 257, 273-4; Vol. 70, pp. 112-3, 250. This view was reiterated by the Congress Working Committee in the resolution by which it took disciplinary action against Subhas Bose for violating party discipline in 1939. Tendulkar, *op. cit.,* Vol. 5, p. 155.

[24]Because of the absence of explicit theory in Gandhi's writings, this entire sub-section is based on our interviews and a 'reading' of the movement. There are however stray remarks of Gandhi on some of the aspects. The interviews are too many to be cited. But those of Achyut Patwardhan, a Working Committee member, and of Madhavalal Shankarlal Pandya and D.K. Kunte, young *taluka* level leaders, are of considerable significance in this respect.

[25]Gandhi's differences with Subhas Bose in 1919 revolved basically on this aspect. Gandhi was convinced that neither the people were yet ready for, nor was the Congress organization in a proper shape to lead, a mass struggle. According to Madhavlal Shankarlal Pandya's understanding, Gandhi went by the people's readiness and not by deduction from theory or by speeches of the leaders. Leaders, said Pandya, always talked tough or bombastically, but the people were different and much more realistic. Similarly, he said that Gandhi decided on a movement's preparedness by looking at the 'strong' areas, e.g., Bardoli, Borsad. If even they were not ready, then the country was not at all.

people, and the Indian state apparatuses were accumulated, and the cadre and activists were unified into a homogeneous and well-disciplined mass.[26] Every effort was made to isolate the 'enemy' by putting him in the wrong and by winning over, uniting with, or neutralizing as many of the non-Congress groups, persons and forces as possible. A constant fight was waged for the soul of the peripheral forces—above all the Liberals and the British Labourites. This was done by three basic tactics. Firstly, all constitutional and legal means for redressal of demands were exhausted. Secondly, constant negotiations were carried on, so that it was the Government that was seen to be blocking a settlement.[27] To drive this home further, the Government was given adequate notice or warning before the launching of the movement. Thirdly, and very importantly, the demands were gradually reduced as the time for the launching of the struggle drew near so that the people—as also observers on the sidelines—increasingly saw that the struggle was being forced upon the national movement, that the people were being left with no choice but to struggle, and that the responsibility for the consequent hardships lay on the shoulders of the Government. But the objective of narrowing down the larger demands to increasingly smaller demands was not done out of weakness, that is, to make a compromise easier and thus to scale down or avoid the struggle. The purpose was that the fight should occur with immense moral and hegemonic reserves on the side of the anti-colonial forces. The struggle over the narrowed down demand was not a partial struggle for a partial demand, it was an integral part, the opening gambit so to speak, of the broader unlimited struggle. It was different from a partial

[26]*Collected Works,* Vol. 68, p. 132. This tactic, so effective in 1930, was blocked by Willingdon in 1931-32 when he struck before Gandhi got a chance to build the movement on his return from Britain. The sudden strike was repeated in August 1942 but Gandhi and the Congress had already done some of the spade work, though not to the needed extent.

[27]This tactic was also blocked by the Willingdon regime in 1931-32 as well as later in 1933-34 when it refused to open negotiations with Gandhi and the Congress leaders.

struggle because it meant confrontation with the authorities all the way. Differentiating the non-payment of land revenue in Bardoli in 1928 from non-payment of revenue in Kheda in 1930, Gandhi wrote: "The Bardoli struggle was in a way limited in scope. It was a fight for securing a right. This is a fight to wrest power from the Government. The one is as far removed from the other as the earth from the sky."[28] In other words, not the extent of demands but the extent of the reserves of hegemony was the issue involved.[29] Moreover, under no circumstances was scaling down to be done if the effect would be to demoralize an aroused people.[30]

Once a movement had been ideologically and politically prepared and then initiated by the leadership or headquarters, the lower level Congress organs and cadre were to carry out the actual movement giving full play to their innovation and initiative. There were only two *a priori* conditions or restrictions: the movement must start only when initiated by the leadership and must stop when the leadership so decided; and that it must remain non-violent.[31] The higher leaders were usually clapped in jail. But even those who remained out acted primarily as coordinators or rather as clearing houses for information. The movement was not only open to initiatives and innovations originating in the mass movement at the ground level, it was crucially dependent upon them. In fact, the Gandhian era movements

[28]*Ibid.*, Vol. 43, pp. 340-1.

[29]The government too saw this aspect. That is why it could not or would not concede even the small demands on which the struggle was ostensibly being fought. Vishwanath Mathur told us that he and his friends had laughed at the idea of making salt the main issue of struggle, but they were totally taken aback at the response the issue evoked among the people.

[30]Gandhi, *Collected Works*, Vol. 69, pp. 317-8, 355-6.

[31]I cannot imagine any organized movement in which the leadership has not or will not insist on the right to initiate or stop the movement or to determine the forms of struggle. The critique of a movement should relate not to the assertion of this right but to its exercise in practice in the concrete and specific historical situations. Apart from laying down the absolute rule regarding non-violence, Gandhi did not try to control a movement at the lower, effective levels. At the most, he gave advice when asked; but even then often stressing the importance of paying attention to local conditions. See his writings on Rajkot and Jaipur struggles during 1939.

were constituted by them.[32] The leadership prepared the movement ideologically and politically, and laid down the main items of the programme of agitation, but seldom made any significant organizational preparation.[33] It would have been in any case difficult to do so for these were open movements whose leadership, organization, and funds were therefore open to immediate Government action. Since Gandhi forbade any secrecy or underground organization, the leadership could not take recourse to them and were completely 'open' to repression. Whatever secret or underground organizational structures developed were at the initiative as well as the level of the local cadre.

Thus, there was full scope for initiative, innovation and creativity at the mass level of the movement; and this was—and was therefore built into—the very structure of a Gandhian movement.

A study of the concrete movements as they were actually waged by the people at the ground level, where alone in any case a mass movement is and can be waged, would reveal immense variety of

[32]This entire relation between leaders and the led was reflected in the nature of relations between the various levels of leaders and followers in the pre-independence Congress. These relations were based on equality, comradeship, mutual regard, absence of hierarchy and freedom to express opposite views. Nearly all our interviewees, including Gandhians, Socialists and Communists, stressed these aspects and strongly refuted the 'patron-client,' 'sub-contractor,' or 'broker' theories of linkages between village level-*taluka* level-district level-and higher level political activists and workers or office holders in the Congress organization.

[33]From 1937 on, CSP and the CPI constantly criticized Gandhi for not preparing for the coming struggle and then tried to find reasons for his failure to do so, the reason most commonly assigned being the bourgeoisie's vacillating character, and tendency to compromise with imperialism or its fear of the masses' militancy. They did not understand that Gandhi was constantly preparing for the coming struggle but in his own way, that preparations for a hegemonic struggle are different from a war of movement or manoeuvre, and that such preparation relates much more to the moral and ideological realm and far less to the realm of organization, except in the sense of mobilization of the people and unification of the masses and cadre into a well-disciplined mass. And throughout 1937- 41, two of Gandhi's main concerns were fighting corruption and lack of discipline within the Congress and solving the communal problem so as to bring about unity among Hindu and Muslim masses. This was his method of 'preparing for struggle.'

ways in which and the issues on which the movement was waged. Unfortunately, the movements have not yet been studied at this level, except by a few like Hiteshranjan Sanyal and Sashi Joshi. Our own statement in this respect is based on our interviews with the freedom fighters from most parts of the country, which have unfortunately not yet been transcribed and therefore fully studied. But to give a few examples. In the second half of 1930 when rains put a virtual end to illegal salt making, it was a young Communist, S.G. Sardesai, who, in the name of the Congress and with an authorization from the Congress leader Shankarrao Deo, innovated and led the Akola Forest Satyagraha. The young D.K. Kunte, a *taluka* level leader in Maharashtra and a staunch Gandhian, heard about it and organized a similar forest *Satyagraha* in Alibagh without the knowledge of or authorization of any higher leader. In fact, *Satyagraha* around salt itself was carried on in different parts of the country in an unlimited variety of ways. Hundreds of *taluka* and district level *patrikas* (illegal news and propaganda bulletins or news-sheets, cyclostyled or hand-copied) came up during 1930-34 as well as 1942-43. From format to content to distribution they were completely 'autonomous.' In the Bardoli and Kheda Satyagrahas, the Chirala-Pirala struggle, and hundreds of other local struggles during the mass movement phases, people gave full play to their diverse creative faculties. Moreover, quite often, if not in almost all cases, after the arrest of the known and tried leaders the movement came under the direction of local, very young and inexperienced activists who perforce had no guidelines to fall back upon and therefore gave full expression to their innovative faculties and youthful zest.[34]

[34]For example, interviews with Umashankar Joshi (Gujarat), Shiv Varma (U.P.), D.K. Kunte (Maharashtra), A.K. Raman Kutty (Palghat), Sri Ram Sharma (Panjab-Haryana), K. Lingaraju (Andhra), and Popatlal Shah (Pune). Sashi Joshi gives numerous examples of the originality and innovation by the lower-cadre. See, Sashi Joshi, *The Left and the Indian National Movement, 1920-34,* Ph.D. Thesis.

In 1942, of course, the leadership officially sanctioned local and individual autonomy of the participants in the coming struggle. The AICC resolution of 8 August 1942 declared that if and when the Congress Committees at all levels cease to function, "every man and woman, who is participating in this movement must function for himself or herself within the four corners of the general instructions issued (by Gandhiji)." But, in fact, this was equally true in practice of the earlier movements, especially in 1930 and 1932-33 when the leadership at the central and provincial levels and often at the district and *taluka* levels was soon put in jail and the Congress organizations declared illegal. This 'autonomous' initiative of the lower level workers and of the masses was not contrary to 'official' Congress strategy, it was an inherent part of it, it was its basic assumption.

CHAPTER 5

Ideological Transformation

A major aspect of the long-term dynamics of the Indian national movement was the struggle by Jawaharlal Nehru, the Congress Socialists, the Communists and other socialist-minded groups and individuals to transform the national movement and the National Congress in a leftward, socialist direction. But what was to be the terrain of this struggle? This was a basic question for it would help decide in whose class interests would the central contradiction with imperialism get resolved as a result of the anti-imperialist struggle, that is, what sort of India would come into existence after independence?

Perhaps, it would be useful to discuss in the beginning as to what this terrain could not—or should not—have been in terms of the concrete, historically specific movement that was sought to be transformed.

It was not a question of transforming the class character, the class essence of a bourgeois national movement or of a bourgeois party, the National Congress, that is, of transforming it from a bourgeois to a proletarian or peasant national movement or party, from a movement in which all the other anti-colonial classes and strata were dominated by or subordinated to the bourgeoisie to a movement in which they were dominated by or subordinated to the working class.[1] The Indian national movement, as an anti-colonial movement, in which the primary contradiction pit the entire society against

[1]This entire question, dealt with in this sub-section, is too large and complex to be discussed here at length. The following remarks may therefore be taken as a brief, preliminary and simplified treatment of the question.

colonialism, was a popular, people's movement, a multi-class mass movement which represented the anti-imperialist interests of all classes and strata. It did not, therefore, have to have a specific, pre-determined, necessary or inevitable or fixed class essence or to bear 'a direct or necessary relationship to classes.'[2]

While anti-colonial nationalism does not arise or function in a social or class vacuum, it does not have to have a specific class belonging, for it represents the primary contradiction of the entire colonial society vis-a-vis colonialism. It is, therefore, incorrect to assume that an anti-colonial national movement serves (or must serve) in practice only one specific class and goes against or does not reflect the interests of another specific class or classes. Such an assumption is particularly untenable when an anti-colonial or national movement has acquired a mass-based character.

This is not to suggest that an anti-colonial movement has no class consequences. Certainly, it is important to the final outcome of the national movement whether the workers, the peasants, the petty bourgeoisie and the intelligentsia play an active part in it. The class consequences of a national movement depend upon the changing balance of political and ideological forces, as also the weight and extent and manner of participation of the different social classes, strata and groups in the movement, particularly at the moment of freedom.[3] One of the tasks of the left trend in a national movement

[2]The problem would be easier to resolve or grasp if the phrase national liberation movement was used in place of national movement. We have not so far heard of the phrase proletarian national movement or proletarian national liberation movement in case of China, Vietnam, Nicaragua or the ex-Portuguese colonies of Africa. The phrase 'peasant nationalism' has never been used by the participants, though the phrase 'peasant nationalism' was coined by some American scholars in case of China basically in order to underplay the roles of socialist ideology and the Communist Party. The phrase is today widely used, but makes sense only as an empirical statement to describe the participation of the peasantry or the role of peasant demands. It has no analytical or historiographic value.

[3]But it is not true that it becomes or remains a bourgeois or upper class movement so long as the proletariat, that is, its political representative—some sort of a Communist Party—does not control it or head it.

is to see that this balance favours the working people and the forces and trends representing them and not the propertied classes and capitalism. The historian has also not to ascribe an historical class essence to a national movement but to study the actual, changing balance of social, political and ideological forces in the course of the development of the concrete historical movement whose objective is, of course, the overthrow of the colonial state.

We do not of course at all agree with those who equate nationalism with bourgeois ideology and maintain that all nationalism or nationalist ideology is *per se* bourgeois in essence; that it can be associated only with the capitalist class; that by its basic character or essence it must serve the bourgeoisie;[4] that nationalism can only be a true ideology for the bourgeoisie and for others it is false consciousness; and that, therefore, the workers and peasants may support or ally with the bourgeoisie in its efforts to unify or free a country or colony but that they themselves cannot and should not be nationalist in ideology and must under no circumstance internalize nationalism, and that their own ideology—at least in the case of workers—can only be socialism, because nationalism is and can only be the ideology of the bourgeoisie.

However, a people, though unified *against* colonialism and *in* the anti-colonial struggle, are at the same time divided into classes. In a

[4]This is very different from saying that nationalism developed in large parts of Europe as a part of the bourgeoisie's ideological ensemble and of its ideological-political struggle against the feudal classes, and that from the last quarter of the 19th century, nationalism has been used by the ruling classes of Europe, USA, and Japan to keep the working classes in a subordinate position despite the existence of adult franchise and political democracy. But this did not happen in Africa and Asia where nationalism was used not by one exploiting class against another but by the entire society against a foreign ruling class. Hence there was no inevitability or universality about the bourgeois character of nationalism. To put it more crudely but dramatically, the nationalism of Gandhi or Mao, Ho Chi Minh or Cabral was totally different from that of Disraeli or Hitler or even Cavour or Bismarck, though it would bear close resemblance to the nationalism embodied in the resistance to Hitler's occupation of France, Italy, Yugoslavia, etc., and in the Soviet people's Great Patriotic War from 1941 to 1945. From the persons we are criticizing we would like to ask whether the French Resistance from 1940 to 1944 in which Communists participated along with De Gaulle was bourgeois in character.

people's or popular movement this division finds reflection in the ideological realm. Several social ideologies function and coexist within a popular, mass national movement. And in various aspects and sometimes in an overall manner some ideological elements or an ideology as a whole occupies a hegemonic position within the overall context of the nationalist ideological hegemony in opposition to colonial ideological hegemony. The socialist transformation project pertains not to the anti-colonial ideological hegemony but to the ideological hegemony within the camp of the people.

To sum up this aspect: A starting point of the project of transforming the national movement, as also of the study of this project, had to be the acceptance of the fact that as a popular mass anti-colonial movement it had to be open-ended, without a fixed class hegemony or a necessary class character. It had to be a multi-class movement rather than a mere alliance of different classes. It was not a movement of the bourgeoisie, national or otherwise, or led or controlled by it. Nor was the National Congress a class party of the bourgeoisie or a united front of the bourgeoisie and landlords, but was a party of the Indian people as a whole including peasants and workers, artisans, the bourgeoisie, the petty bourgeoisie, the intelligentsia, and sections of landlords. Nationalism, or anti-imperialism, in a colony did not represent only the ideology of the bourgeoisie or express only the bourgeoisie's contradiction with imperialism. It represented the entire colonial society's contradiction with imperialism. In other words, the national movement or the National Congress did not bear a direct or necessary or inevitable relation to the bourgeoisie or the bourgeois class structure.

II

In our view, there was also no need to locate the transformation on the terrains of strategy, forms of struggle, mass character of the movement, militancy and the anti-imperialist character of the Indian national movement. The strategy and forms of struggle and organization have, in our view, no class essence. As we have argued above, non-violence as an ideology or non-violent *Satyagraha*, law-breaking, picketing, mass meetings, illegal processions, *jathas,* morchas, etc., or the S-T-S′ strategy, were not articulated to or associated with the practice of particular classes, there was nothing specifically bourgeois about them. In fact, the Indian bourgeoisie as a class did not associate itself with many of the forms of struggle adopted by the national movement. At the most, it took part in fund-collection and hartals, which were at no stage declared illegal by the Government.[5] Nor has the bourgeoisie of any country shown much aversion to violence or a dedication to non-violence in any part of the world. The question of whether the forms of struggle or the S-T-S′ strategy were necessarily the best or even adequate under the specific circumstances of colonial India and whether they should not have been replaced with better ones was not one that could be discussed in terms of socialist vs. capitalist or left vs. right. It did not relate to socialist transformation but to the manner of the waging of the national struggle; socialist transformation did not necessarily require transformation of strategy and forms of struggle. If the latter was needed, it was on other grounds. The Right and the Left could be and were on either side of the strategic debate and could and did also change their positions without affecting their ideologies—as did Nehru in 1937. Also the Left-Right demarcation did not pertain to the character of the national movement as a mass movement—the Right was as much committed to this character as the Left—, or to the political militancy of the movement.[6] There might be differences on the questions of when to go over to more militant

[5]Aditya Mukherjee, "The Indian Capitalist Class: Aspects of its Economic, Political and Ideological Development in the Colonial Period."

[6]This was sometimes articulated by the members of the Congress Right. See, for example, Rajendra Prasad in his presidential address to the Congress in 1934: "The method is crystal clear. It is active dynamic non-violent mass action." Quoted in Tendulkar, *op. cit.,* Vol. 3, p. 302. What is more, the Right at no stage lagged behind in militancy or mass mobilization once the decision to launch a mass movement was taken. We may also

forms or to extra-legal mass movement, or how to work the existing constitutional machinery, but on these questions the Left and the Right were often divided within themselves. There was also, we believe, no difference on the degree of commitment to anti-imperialism.[7] There could not be a more serious error than locating the right-wingness of the Right in its approach to imperialism, or in assuming that it had a tendency to 'bargain,' 'collaborate' and 'compromise with' or 'surrender to' imperialism. The Right, as much as the Left, was committed to consistent and determined anti-imperialism.

III

The project of a leftward transformation of the national movement could also not relate to or be directed towards the Congress policy of treating the internal contradictions of Indian society as secondary and therefore advocating and practising class adjustment rather than an all-out class war on landlords and capitalists. We believe that acceptance of two basic ideas, *(a)* of a society being divided into mutually hostile classes waging class struggle against each other and *(b)* of colonial domination and exploitation leading to a primary contradiction between the colonial people and colonialism, opened up a fresh terrain in the history of colonial society and nationalism. If these two ideas are placed together, their inter-relationship understood, and the significance of class adjustment in a colonial

not forget that Sardar Patel led more militant mass movements of the peasants than probably any other of his contemporaries. The big difference between the Left and the Right on these two questions related to perceptions of people's readiness to struggle. Most on the Left believed that the masses were always ready for militant mass action and that too for an indefinite period. Most on the Right believed that there were times when masses were so ready and times when they were not. Interestingly, the practice of the Left in the trade union and peasant struggles they led approximated very closely to that of the Right except in the nature of class issues taken up and the ideological dimensions of their work. This has been affirmed by most of the left leaders and activists we have interviewed.

[7] I have discussed these aspects in another article, "Struggle for the Ideological Transformation of the National Congress in the 1930s," in *Ideology and Politics in Modern India.*

society fighting for national liberation realized, a fresh focus may be provided for looking into, and grasping dimensions hitherto neglected in, the study of the anti-colonial struggle and the role of class struggle in the colonial context. We may therefore make a longish detour.

Class division and class exploitation would indicate that a basic task of the Left was to organize the workers and peasants in class organizations and to fight for their class demands through popular struggles around them. At the same time, the primacy of the primary contradiction meant that the Indian exploiters and the exploited were members of the same camp of the anti-colonial people. The problem was how to combine class struggles with the primacy of the anti-colonial struggle. Clearly, inner class contradictions had to be seen as secondary and therefore subordinated to the primary contradictions; they had to be seen as contradictions within the camp of the people, and class struggles based on them had to be waged in a non-antagonistic fashion. This would mean not pushing class struggles within Indian society to their limits. *It would mean making class compromises and class adjustments among the mutually hostile Indian social classes.* Though Congress, and in particular Gandhi, practised the strategy of class adjustment,[8] to our knowledge no Indian leader, not even Gandhi, theorized it. The Marxist leaders of the nationalist movements, on the other hand, not only practised it but also put it in an explicit programmatic form during the 1930s. In the face of the imperialist enemy, they argued, class struggle was to be adjusted, with all mutually hostile classes within the colonial or semi-colonial society making concessions to one another. The classical Marxist position in this respect, though initiated by Marx and Engels,[9] was fully developed by Mao Ze Dong during the anti-Japanese struggle of the Chinese people.[10]

[8]Francine Frankel, *India's Political Economy 1947-1977,* pp. 35 ff.

[9]*Ireland and the Irish Question.*

[10]Dong, Mao Ze, *Selected Works,* Vol. Two, p. 264.

> To subordinate the class struggle to the present national struggle to resist Japan—that is the fundamental principle of the united front.... In a nation which is struggling against a foreign foe, the class struggle assumes the form of national struggle, a form indicating the consistency of the two. On the one hand, the economic and political demands of the classes during the historical period of national struggle should be based on the condition of not disrupting the cooperation of these classes; on the other, all the demands of the class struggle should start from the requirements of the national struggle.

And again:[11]

> It is a settled principle that in the anti-Japanese War everything must be subordinated to the interests of resistance to Japan. Therefore the interests of the class struggle must not conflict with, but be subordinated to, the interests of the War of Resistance. But the classes and class struggle do exist.... *We do not deny the class struggle, but adjust it....* In order to unite against Japan we should carry out a suitable policy that can adjust the class relations.

Mao also explained what he meant by class adjustment:[12]

> The workers should demand that the factory owners improve their material conditions, but at the same time they should work hard in order to facilitate resistance to Japan; the landlords should reduce rent and interest, but at the same time the peasants should pay rent and interest to the landlords and unite with them against foreign aggression.

The Vietnamese Communists too practised and wrote about class adjustment in the same fashion.[13] Interestingly enough, the

[11] *Ibid.*, p. 250. (Emphasis added).

[12] *Ibid.*, p. 263.

[13] For details of their stand as also Mao Ze Dong's, see Bhagwan Josh, "Ministries and the Left."

Communist Party of India too practised class adjustment during the period of People's War once they located the primary contradiction in the anti-fascist struggle on a world scale.[14] Moreover, unlike Mao and the Chinese Communist Party, the CPI adjusted the class struggle in an empiricist fashion without theorizing it in terms of the relation between primary and secondary contradictions or antagonistic and non-antagonistic contradictions. We may also note that Sahajanand Saraswati who would not give an iota of concession to or make any accommodation with the Congress Ministry during 1937-39 was openly asking the peasants not to struggle against the zamindars during 1942-44.

The point of contention had to be not class adjustment, which was bound to be a part of the anti-colonial paradigm, but the terms on which it was to be made and the manner in which class struggle was viewed and provided for within the parameters of colonial society and the anti-imperialist struggle. What was also important was the ideology that underlay class adjustment. Class adjustment was also not to be seen as something fixed. Its contours, its terms were to be seen as constantly shifting through conscious effort. For example, on the agrarian front, abolition of *begar* (forced labour) and end to evictions could be the initial points of adjustment, later rent reduction could be incorporated and in the end even the issue of abolition of landlordism could be posed with compromise taking the form of compensation to the landlords. The terms of class adjustment would depend on the levels of peasants' consciousness, mobilization, organization and struggle and the extent to which the movement as a whole had shifted leftwards. In

[14]This is what P.C. Joshi, the then General Secretary of the CPI, wrote to Gandhi in 1945 regarding the party's class struggle policy during the War. "We gave up our strike policy because we considered it anti-national in the conditions of the day.... That we successfully prevented the Indian working class from resorting to strikes even in a period of their worsening material conditions is the measure not only of our influence over it but its capacity to *understand* national interests as its own." *Correspondence between Mahatma Gandhi and P.C. Joshi*, p. 12.

other words, the Right was to be criticized and opposed when it objected to organization of the exploited classes or class struggles around their class demands or opposed the ideology of class struggle but not when it proposed class adjustment and confining of class struggles within the parameters of broad unity of all sections of the Indian people.

Interestingly, the Right agreed at Karachi in 1931 and after to the organization of the Indian masses into their various class organizations such as trade unions and kisan sabhas—it even organized them in its own way especially when facing the colonial state or foreign enterprises. It also did not object to struggles around the class demands of the workers and peasants even when internal exploiters were involved.[15] But it precisely said that class struggles should be adjusted and fought for in a non-antagonistic manner and therefore without physical violence against the internal exploiters or without being pushed to the extreme of demanding their liquidation as a class. Consequently, it agreed, though often under pressure of the Left, to the embodiment of increasingly radical, though adjusted, class demands—demands on this side of the total liquidation of class exploitation and exploiters—within the Congress programme at Karachi and Faizpur and in the Election Manifesto of 1937. It also agreed to have supporters of class struggles as Presidents from 1936 to 1938 and as members of the Working Committee.[16] If we keep in view the constraint of time, the record of the Congress Ministries in adjusting the class balance in favour of the peasants via agrarian and other reforms was quite radical. Even the more conservative Bihar legislation provided for 25 per cent reduction in land rent.[17]

[15]For example, in Gujarat, Sardar Patel and others in the 1930s supported Halpatis—bonded labourers—in their fight against bondage. In 1931, Sardar Patel as president of the Congress and Gandhi sanctioned the no-rent campaign in U.P.

[16]These steps have often been seen as right manoeuvres or the Right's efforts to co-opt or bamboozle the Left. A better explanation is that the Right recognized the need to build a wider popular movement based on class adjustment, etc.

[17]To quote B.B. Chaudhuri: "Rent was reduced by about 25 per cent, on an average. Peasants' holdings were made transferable without the prior consent of zamindars,

A good example of class adjustment is to be found in Gandhi's manifesto 'To the Kisans' of U.P. in May 1931. The manifesto asked the peasants to pay only 75 or 50 per cent of the rent. In case of inability to pay even this, they could reduce the rent further:[18]

> The Congress expects every tenant to pay as early as possible all the rent he can, and in no case as a general rule less than 8 annas or 12 annas as the case may be. But just as even in the same district there may be cases in which a larger payment is possible, it is equally possible that there may be cases in which less than 8 annas or 12 annas can only be paid. In such cases I hope the tenants will be treated liberally by the zamindars. In every case you will see that you get against payment a full discharge from your obligation for the current year's rent.

A very good example of combining agrarian radicalism, class adjustment and anti-colonialism, which was virtually Mao-like in its conception, were the draft instructions for civil resisters prepared by Gandhi on 4 August 1942 and discussed by the Congress Working Committee on 8 August. After laying down that "the Congress holds that the land belongs to those who work on it and to no one else," the instructions said that where a zamindar joined hands with the ryot in refusing to pay land tax the zamindar should be paid his portion of the revenue but if he sided with the Government, "no tax should be paid to him."[19] Echoes of Mao's 'patriotic landlords!'

and the salami that was previously payable to them at the time of such transfers was greatly reduced. Sales by zamindars of the entire holdings of peasants on grounds of non-payment of due rent were made illegal. Zamindars could sell only a part of the holdings, which was enough for the realization of the arrears of rent. The Ministry persuaded the zamindars to agree not only to a reduction of the cash rent, but also of the share of the crop." "Agrarian Movements in Bengal and Bihar, 1919-1939," in A.R. Desai, *op. cit.*, p. 364. During the Anti-Japanese War, Mao too recommended a rent reduction of 25 per cent. *Selected Works*, Vol. Three, p. 221.

[18] *Collected Works*, Vol. 46, p. 201 with correction on p. 350.

[19] *Ibid.*, Vol. 76, p. 367.

Then, there was the specific demand for the abolition of landlordism without compensation. The right-wing was, again wrongly, defined as all those who opposed this demand. In semi-colonial semi-feudal countries like China, where state power is shared or even largely wielded by domestic classes, mainly landlords and compradors, the political objectives of the struggle alternate. Sometimes the struggle against feudalism and for liquidation of landlordism becomes primary because, while remaining an enemy, colonialism *is not* and *cannot* become the target of the immediate and main political movement for arousal of the people and struggle for state power. Examples are the Chinese struggle from 1922 to 1934, whose direct targets were the warlords with their social base among the landlords, and the Civil War, 1946-49, whose task was the overthrow of Chiang Kai-shek's power. In both cases, agrarian revolution took the centre of the stage. On the other hand, when colonialism directly threatens or rules, the colonial state or colonial state-to-be becomes the immediate target of mass mobilization and the struggle for abolition of landlordism is either not taken up or abandoned. This was the case in China in 1918-19 and 1937-45 and in Vietnam after 1939.

In India, colonialism ruled directly; none of the Indian social classes shared in state power.[20] Therefore, the liquidation of feudalism or agrarian revolution as an immediate slogan was invalid throughout and could only be a long-term goal. The bourgeois democratic stage of revolution was directed against feudalism in Europe; in India the equivalent stage had to be directed against colonialism. The mixing up of anti-colonial and agrarian revolution here was a mixing up of recipes, not good for the health of the national movement or the Left. And, as we have pointed out earlier, the Right agreed to go quite far vis-a-vis landlordism (and usury), short of its liquidation.

[20] See my "Colonialism, Stages of Colonialism and the Colonial State."

IV

In our view the chief terrain for the transformation of the national movement and the Congress in a socialist direction was the ideological including the moral and intellectual. Indian nationalism from the 1880s onwards was firmly rooted in a correct critique of the character of the colonial economy based on a perspective of independent modern economic development. This development perspective, however, remained largely confined within bourgeois parameters, or, independent economic development was visualized within a capitalist framework. Thus we may characterize the movement or the Congress as a popular or people's movement that was under bourgeois ideological hegemony or rather under the hegemony of bourgeois economic ideology.[21] After 1919, when the national movement became a mass movement, Gandhi evolved and propagated a different, non-capitalist, basically peasantist-artisanist outlook but his socio-economic programme or economic thought were not capable of challenging the basic hegemony of bourgeois ideology.

Thus it was the national movement's social vision of a free India or the bourgeois ideological hegemony that had to be transformed by the Left through continuous and intense ideological struggle. The issue may be put in another manner. The question here was not whether one would be a bourgeois nationalist or proletarian nationalist; the question was—would one be a nationalist from the bourgeois perspective of social development or from the socialist point of view. There are, however, several important implications of the terrain of struggle being ideological in case of a popular, mass anti-colonial movement. The effort or struggle was to be for the establishment of the hegemony of socialist ideas over the entire anti-

[21]We are not fully satisfied with this concept or formulation. It is, we realize, quite ambiguous and perhaps even crude. But we have to rely upon it till we have examined the entire problem in detail on some other occasion. At this stage we may only add a qualification. The concept should be taken in its 'weak' and not 'strong' sense.

imperialist movement and above all in or over the Congress. The project was not to be that of winning over only the working class and the poor and middle peasantry; or of transforming the Congress into a class party of the workers, etc.; or of constructing class alliances between different classes already represented by their own parties: or of establishing proletarian hegemony over the Congress; or of capturing its leadership at different levels. The socialist alternative was to be posed not in terms of the leadership of the movement by the working class or by a working class party but in ideological terms, that is, as a moral and intellectual and social developmental alternative and not as a class alternative. The task was to give the movement a new socialist ideological orientation and not to struggle to create alternatives to the existing national movement or to Gandhi's leadership.

Through patient and friendly argument and persuasion, carried out orally and in writing, and through the example of practice, nationalists, especially nationalist political workers, of all hues and from all sections of society were to be converted to socialism as a historical and societal objective; and the task was not very difficult because they were already oriented towards and committed to broader social ideals and objectives.[22] The struggle for transformation had to be woven primarily not around corporatist class demands or interests—though the struggle around them was to be undertaken as a part of class work among the masses—but around societal objectives and above all around ideas and ideologies. The task was to affect the social ideology preached by the national workers day after day and on which popular agitation was based. The task was not to concentrate on deciding which class was represented by which leader or political group but to popularize socialist ideas among all those open to their acceptance. The task was not to look for *de novo*

[22] Our interviews indicate that throughout the 1930s and early 1940s the left political workers were having a strong impact on non-left Congressmen because of their selfless work and militant anti-imperialism.

beginnings or to create 'ready-made' radical forces according to a well-prepared schema but to incorporate and develop further existing radicalism or the historically evolved radical forces and currents till they were ready for a qualitative leap—this is what happened in Cuba, Nicaragua, Portuguese colonies in Africa, and above all in China (vis-a-vis the 4 May Movement, Sun Yat-sen and Kuomintang, the Anti-Japanese Resistance). The task was to constantly work for establishing a more radical balance or equilibrium of existing forces.[23] To use more recent terminology, ideological transformation meant changing the balance of existing nationalist discourses.[24] It was also to be realized that transformation of a movement or an organization like the Congress is a process and not an event and as a process it had to develop stage by stage. We may note that as part of its transformation, the Congress progressively evolved in a radical social direction and increasingly accepted most of the demands put forward by the Left though with a time lag of a few years. The politics of the Left and workers' and peasants' struggles, of course, played a critical role in this evolution. For the task of transformation to be successfully undertaken, it was also necessary to develop a correct understanding of the existing national movement led by the Congress and to develop a correct relationship with it.[25]

From the socialist point of view, the primacy of ideological struggle under colonial conditions had one other aspect. Since no anti-colonial movement could take up the task of the abolition of private property, the socialist project could not be given a

[23]Different ideological currents had still to be there. Transformation did not mean making the movement a single-tracked one. A multi-class movement could not possibly accept in name or reality the full programme of one component class. Only the weight of the movement had to be constantly shifted in a radical direction, without demanding or accepting a monopoly or hegemony for one particular current.

[24]See Ernesto Laclau, *Politics and Ideology in Marxist Theory*.

[25]Otherwise, they would not only fail to establish socialist hegemony over the national movement but find it difficult to make much headway in creating and establishing their influence over the class organizations of workers and peasants.

programmatic shape except in the ideological realm. A multi-class movement could only accept a socialist vision and not an immediate proletarian class programme—to try to do so was to mix stages. Thus, so long as colonial rule persisted, there could be no struggle for the realization of socialism, only struggle for the spread of socialist ideology and for the ideological transformation of the national liberation struggle.

V

Thus, we believe that despite the limitations of their existing ideology the Indian national movement and the National Congress which led it were quite open to transformation towards a socialist perspective or vision. This possibility existed because of several features of the situation and the movement.

(i) The very fact that the national movement was an anti-colonial mass movement made it open-ended, without any one class as a class hegemonizing it.[26] Precisely because its class content or class character took the form not of direct class domination or class leadership but of ideological hegemony made it open to ideological transformation or the replacement of one ideological hegemony by another. Moreover, Right and Left were part of a wide ideological spectrum and not its nodal points. In these respects, the Congress was much more akin to the British Labour Party which has not been a socialist party but has also not been a bourgeois party or a party under bourgeois leadership. It has been a party under bourgeois ideological hegemony.[27] That is why it has been possible for extreme

[26]The underlying and well understood assumption of the leading representatives of the capitalist class—men like G.D. Birla and Purshottamdas Thakurdas—in their relationship with the Congress was precisely this that the Congress did not belong to or represent the interests of the capitalist class or any other single class. It was the complex understanding of the Indian National Congress by the capitalist class which facilitated the maintenance of bourgeois ideological hegemony over the national movement, despite strong contending hegemonies within it. See Aditya Mukherjee, *op. cit.*

[27]Partha Sarathi Gupta has recently described it as a working class movement under reformist ideological hegemony.

radicals and Marxists, fully committed to socialism, to join it They have done so, over the years as also at present, not with the conviction that it was or is a socialist party but on the basis that it was capable of being transformed in or shifted towards a socialist direction.[28]

(ii) Ideological transformation was not to be a new experience for the Congress. It had been undergoing such transformation as well as struggle since the 1880s. In fact, it was founded as a result of ideological contention, by the younger nationalists led by Dadabhai Naoroji, regarding the character of colonialism and the anti-colonial movement. The early years of the 20th century and the 1920s were to witness fierce struggles within it on ideological issues.

(iii) Though bourgeois ideological hegemony penetrated deep and acquired wide acceptance because it held ground for a very long time, nevertheless it was not very consciously or fully or even strongly structured on a class basis. It was never very 'hard,' i.e., it never assumed a fully crystallized form. It was adopted and reigned supreme from the 1880s till 1917 because of the relative absence or weak availability of any other path of development in India and not because of the founding fathers' commitment to capitalism or the capitalist class. The Moderates had to look for Indian agents of independent industrial development, otherwise they could not structure a critique of colonial economy, especially as colonial economists and other ideologues constantly pointed to the relative absence of any other agents of modern industrial development except foreign capitalists. In the absence of their 'thinking' and putting forward alternative Indian class agents or instruments of development, their entire critique would have been purely abstract, hanging in a social vacuum and lacking in viability and appeal. The

[28]As we shall see, the one big difference is that the Congress permitted all political and ideological trends to join, even if they were committed to bringing about socialism through violent revolution and belonged to revolutionary parties of their own, and so on, while the Labour Party does not permit Trotskyists, Communists and believers in Marxism-Leninism and violent over-throw of the state to join it.

alternative to looking up to an indigenous capitalist class would have been to look to the colonial state; otherwise how could modern industry have been initiated? To think of socialism in the absence of modern industry would have been a pure intellectual pastime or luxury. And Moderates were men of action. This is how the Moderates—radical intellectuals of their time—came to acquire Indian capitalists as the class agents or carriers of their anti-colonial programme or project as also the belief, correct at the time, that the interests of Indian capital were broadly congruent with the interests of the nation. The dominant elements of their ideological discourse were anti-colonialism or nationalism and independent economic development; bourgeois ideology was a subsidiary element.[29] Gandhi did not do so, but then, because his basic ideology was also formed in the pre-1917 period, he looked to the small artisans and the peasantry for alternative non-colonial economic development. And when he was forced to recognize the necessity of modern large-scale industry, he opted for state ownership of such industry.[30] It was only with the emergence of actual historical socialism, especially its developmental side through Soviet planning, that different class agents and paths of modern industrial development could be concretely 'thought.' Consequently, once the socialist perspective emerged after the October Revolution and the foundations of modern industry had been laid, this perspective did not meet strong intellectual resistance from the nationalists and not only did the emerging Left become an accepted part of the national movement

[29]Thus their chief concern was not 'bourgeois'; it was not to serve the capitalist class or to develop it as a class but to develop the Indian economy the only way they thought it could be developed at the time. They were therefore bourgeois intellectuals and not bourgeois leaders, not to speak of bourgeois agents. See my *The Rise and Growth of Economic Nationalism in India,* Chapter XV. Interestingly, when they found the class agents of their anti-colonial project not coming forth in large enough numbers, they themselves tried to assume the role, usually suffering large losses in the process. *Ibid.,* pp. 85-8.

[30]He said this often enough. For an early expression of this view in 1924, see *Collected Works,* Vol. 25, p. 251.

and its ideological spectrum but the socialist perspective was able to grow rapidly, winning over a large number of adherents among the nationalist workers. No major school of thought among the nationalists was to put up a strong defence of capitalism as a system. For example, in the National Planning Committee, the overwhelming bias among the non-capitalist members was against capitalism and for socialism.

(iv) The basic pro-people or pro-poor orientation of the national movement from its inception and the notion that politics must be based on the people, who must be politicized, activised and brought into politics, as brought out above, also made it easier to give it a socialist orientation.

A very positive feature of the Congress was its ideological and organizational open-endedness. As the broad anti-imperialist movement of the entire Indian people and not only of one class or stratum, it could not be and was not ideologically homogeneous. It included within its ranks widely divergent ideological and political tendencies which could freely compete and contend within it for acceptance by the mass of Congressmen. The Congress never laid down any ideological condition for joining it;[31] nor did Gandhi claim any ideological or policy monopoly over it.[32] Even those ideological currents were permitted to function within it which were committed to capturing or transforming it or which stood out as alternatives to it. The Communists, Socialists and Royists were permitted to work within it, while they were simultaneously organizing the workers and peasants in trade unions and kisan sabhas which were not a part of the Congress. Large number of Revolutionaries of Anushilan Samiti and other similar organisations were active Congress workers and functionaries. The Communists,

[31]In the Gandhian era, the only conditions laid down for becoming a part of the Congress were non-violence as a tactic (not necessarily as a principle) and permission from the higher leadership for starting a mass movement in the name of the Congress.

[32]We have already cited above Gandhi's praise for the Communists' courage in taking an honest independent stand on the crucial 1942 August Resolution.

for example, functioned within the Congress, participated in its organizational elections, often became members of the AICC and held high offices at the district and provincial planes. At no stage was Communist dissidence undemocratically suppressed. In 1929 they on their own walked out of the Congress; and they were permitted to rejoin it at will. Communists were barred from holding office in the Congress only in late 1945 not because they represented workers or were Marxists but on the ground that following their party line they had broken the movement's discipline by refusing to join and even opposing a life-and-death anti-imperialist struggle launched by the parent body. And even then they were not barred from the primary membership of the Congress.

(v) We may also note that the leadership of the national movement did not at any stage give way to contemporary right-wing ideologies. The Revolution of 1917 was given warm welcome by Tilak and most of the other national leaders. The Soviet Union was admired and supported throughout. The left cultural currents of Europe, Asia and Americas had an immediate impact. For example, Gorky's *Mother* was translated in Indian languages by Congressmen in the late 1920s and early 1930s and was one of the most widely read books of the time. The Congress supported anti-imperialist movements irrespective of the political colour of their leadership. Marxism found a ready welcome and no strong anti-Marxist intellectual current developed in the nationalist ranks till 1947. Interestingly, at no stage did a break in the Congress occur over ideology.

This ideological openness not only enhanced the possibility of transforming the Congress, it was also a feature which made the Congress a political expression of the historic bloc of all anti-colonial classes and forces, and which in turn constituted them as the Indian people and made the Congress a popular movement. This feature also enabled the Congress to wage a prolonged hegemonic and mass struggle against colonialism. After all a major strategic aspect of such a struggle is the need to keep all people with a common objective and basic values united so long as there is a minimum agreement.[33]

(vi) Within the constraints of bourgeois developmental perspective, the movement and the Congress adopted increasingly radical socio-economic-political programme and policies. This is brought out in Chapter 2 above.

(vii) The intermediate, popular ideological positions of Gandhi and his dominant position in the national movement were quite favourable to the socialist ideological transformation of the Congress. Gandhi did not accept class analysis of society and the role of class struggle; nor was he a socialist in the Marxist sense of the term and several times opposed communism 'for its violence.' His basic outlook was, however, that of social transformation. He was committed to basic changes in the existing system of economic and political power, though he hoped to bring them about in a non-class way and without overt class struggle. Moreover, he was constantly moving in a radical direction during the 1930s and 1940s. Judging from his overall ideological framework and his stand on economic, social and political issues during this latter period, it can be said that he was certainly intellectually or ideologically not a bourgeois[34] and had very many ideological, programmatic and policy positions in common with the Left. We have given an example of his agrarian radicalism above in Chapter 2. He was also beginning to oppose private property[35] and repeatedly argued for nationalization of large-scale industry. His stand on these questions and on exploitation

[33]Cf. Gandhi in 1939: "In any case satyagraha through a majority is not a feasible proposition. The whole weight of the Congress should be behind any nation-wide satyagraha." *Collected Works,* Vol. 69, p. 361.

[34]In class terms, his ideology may be defined as peasantist-cum-artisanist or Utopian socialist, with many of the weak and strong points of Utopian socialism. To describe him as ideologically bourgeois is to suggest that anyone who is not a Marxist is a bourgeois.

[35]Gandhi's theory of trusteeship, opposite of Marxism, was certainly a major lacuna in this respect. But it was not used by him to justify the existing pattern of property relations and he constantly developed it in a more radical direction, using it in the end to justify the idea of land to the tiller.

inherent in capitalism and landlordism, his stand on the relation between physical and mental labour, his general and frequent emphasis on the self-activity of the masses and on social and economic equality, on workers' role in the freedom struggle, against untouchability and for women's social liberation, on civil liberties, and his general awareness of social problems[36] prevented the strong structuring of bourgeois ideology over the national movement and created constant openings for any pro-poor, socially progressive ideology and for cooperation between Gandhi, Gandhians and the Left. It is also important to remember that his ideas and activity did not restrain the masses or pacify them; they aroused and activised them. Moreover, with the presence of all the radical themes in it, and with its orientation towards the lowly, the exploited and the down-trodden, Gandhi's own overall social ideology was open to development and transformation in a socialist direction, though he did not himself articulate them into a coherent socialist world view. In any case, we believe, that the situation was favourable for the Left to interact with Gandhi, his thought and the Gandhian cadre, and, through ideological struggle, based on a serious study and analysis of Gandhi and Gandhians and their writings and social practices, to shape the national movement in a socialist direction.

(viii) Bourgeois ideological hegemony was represented in the Congress by a Right which held a powerful position in its organizational structure at the middle and top levels. But a systematic analysis of the components of the Right's ideology would indicate that it was not a very formidable barrier at the ideological level to the socialist project. Firstly, the Congress Right was, as pointed out earlier, firmly nationalist and committed to an extra-legal mass struggle against imperialism, a civil libertarian, secular and democratic polity, an independent economy, opposition to

[36]The references would be too many. We will leave the task of elaborating this aspect to some other occasion. The readers may see Gyorgy Kalmar, *Gandhism;* and Francine Frankel, *op. cit.,* Chapters 1 and 2.

foreign capital, and an independent and anti-colonial foreign policy. Secondly, in their social ideology, they were bourgeois, but in a reformist way. For example, in their agrarian outlook, they represented the viewpoint and interests of the landowning peasants and not of the zamindars, landlords and moneylenders.[37] Comparisons across time and space tend to be deceptive, but we might still say that though committed to private property and opposed to socialism and class struggle, their ideological and programmatic stance or position did not resemble that of the Tories of Britain, or Bismarckian and later reactionaries of Germany, the makers of Meiji Japan, Cavour and other leaders of post-unification Italy, or the Republicans and Democrats of the USA. They, of course, bore no resemblance to the 20th century European Right. They were more radical than the 19th century Radical Liberals of Britain or the late 19th century Progressives of the USA. They were much more akin to the post-Second World War Social Democrats of Western Europe or the New Dealers of Roosevelt in the USA. In fact, it may be said that the European-style conservatives and rightists were to be found only on the fringe of the Congress and among the Liberals, etc., who functioned outside the Congress. Similarly, the zamindars and land-lords did not support the Congress except individually, but either supported Aman Sabhas and similar officially-sponsored organizations or had, as was the case in Punjab, U.P., Bihar and Madras, their own political parties.

One result was that on the concrete items of socio-economic and political programme, most of the leaders of the Right were willing to go quite far in accommodating the Left so long as it remained within the parameters of class adjustment and peaceful change. Another was that they were willing to cooperate closely with Nehru

[37]Hardly any work has been done on the social ideology of the Congress Right. Neerja Singh has taken up the project. See her preliminary study, "The Right and the Right-Wing Politics in the Congress: 1934-1939," M. Phil. dissertation.

and work alongside the Socialists and the Communists in the freedom struggle.[38]

(ix) The overwhelming majority of the Congress cadre at lower levels were not committed socialists or Marxists but were not ideologically right-wing either, even when they were organizationally aligned with one or the other leader of the Right. In fact, our interviews show that throughout the 1920s, 1930s and 1940s, the scope of popular politics based on wide popular demands was growing and the nationalist cadre were increasingly turning to socialist ideas and a socialist vision of a free India, This was also true of Gandhian workers who had a lot in common with the socialist and communist workers and were inclined towards a socialist and anti-feudal programme provided the Gandhian strategy and emphasis on non-violence were not questioned. This fact is important because *in the long run* it is the political and ideological trends at the grassroots level which would be decisive and not what happened in the Working Committee or the Provincial Committees. The radicalization was then increasingly reflected, as we have shown in Chapter 2 above, in the Congress policies and programme and the growing weight of the CSP and the CPI within the Congress organization.

(x) The Left had a few other positive factors working in its favour. Despite certain weaknesses in Jawaharlal Nehru, a major one being a certain lack of organizational ability or perhaps a disinclination to devote himself to the humdrum of organizational work, in him the Left had an outstanding leader who was, next to Gandhi, the most popular leader in the country. Even if not an original thinker, he was a great publicist, an indefatigable speaker and campaigner, a successful popularizer, and a darling of the youth. Above all, he had an instinctive grasp of the correct approach towards the problem of the ideological transformation of the Congress and the national

[38] The level of cooperation between the leftists and the rightists was even greater among lower level workers. Most of our interviewees have testified to this.

movement. Throughout the 1930s, he pointed to the inadequacy of the existing nationalist ideology and the hegemony of the propertied classes over it and stressed the need to inculcate a new socialist or basically Marxist ideology, which would enable the people to study their condition scientifically, to give the Congress a new ideological orientation. He worked hard to win over others in the Congress to the new ways of thought. Several chapters of his *Autobiography*, written during 1934-35, were an ideological polemic against Gandhi but couched in a mild, friendly, even reverential tone. At the same time he defended the Congress from hostile criticism from the Left, stressing the importance as well as the possibilities of giving it a socialist orientation and of its transformation in a socialist direction.[39]

The Left was able to recruit to its leadership other individuals who were outstanding by any reckoning; and it was able to attract into its ranks cadre with great intelligence, immense capacity and courage, loyalty, devotion and dedication, staunchness and spirit of sacrifice. The roster of the Left leaders of the pre-independence period includes Jawaharlal Nehru, Acharya Narendra Dev, Bhagat Singh, Subhas Bose, M.N. Roy, S.A. Dange, P. Krishna Pillai, P. Sundarayya, Jayaprakash Narayan, Rammanohar Lohia, G. Adhikari, Ajoy Ghosh, Bhagat Singh Bilga, Sohan Singh Josh, Sohan Singh Bakhna, Teja Singh Swatantra, R.D. Bhardwaj, P.C. Joshi, E.M.S. Namboodripad, Muzaffar Ahmed, Sajjad Zaheer, Z.A. Ahmad, B.T. Ranadive, K.M. Ashraf, K. Damodaran, Swami Sahajanand Saraswati, N.G. Ranga, Aruna Asaf Ali, Satyavati, Kamaladevi Chattopadhyaya, Achyut Patwardhan, Rahul Sankritayan, Karyanand Sharma, A.K. Gopalan, and countless others of a similar calibre.

VI

Ideological transformation of the Congress was put on the agenda during the late 1920s and 1930s, and the project achieved partial

[39]See S. Gopal, *Jawaharlal Nehru, A Biography*, Volume One, especially pp. 181, 213-4. and 218 for a brilliant summing up of Nehru's position regarding the ideological transformation of the Congress.

success rather rapidly. The impact of the Russian Revolution of 1917 was felt widely and immediately and a left current developed from the early 1920s within the ranks of the national movement. Beginning with the late 1920s, bourgeois ideological hegemony over the national movement was challenged in a serious manner by early Communist groups, Jawaharlal Nehru, Subhas Chandra Bose, and socialist-minded individuals. The ideological struggle was intensified in the 1930s when these were joined by the Congress Socialist Party, a reorganized Communist Party and the Royists. Nehru's speeches and writings during 1933-36 played a vanguardist role in this process. The Great Depression in the capitalist world, the success of the Soviet Five-Year Plans, the anti-fascist wave the world over, and the turn to Marxism among many British intellectuals were also major positive influences. Leaders of the youth movement of the late 1920s and of the volunteers of the Civil Disobedience Movement (CDM) turned to socialism under these influences and also because the collapse of the CDM in 1932-33 and its replacement by constructive work and parliamentary activity after 1934 raised doubts in them about the effectiveness of the Gandhian style of politics. Almost all young intellectuals brought up during the 1930s turned towards socialism of one type or another. The rising peasant movements and trade unions, too, increasingly moved left. The Congress Socialists and the Communists after 1935 became active members of the Congress. Nehru stomped the country propagating socialism, and the Congress was increasingly radicalised. This radicalization found expression in the Karachi Resolution in 1931, Nehru's Presidential Address to the Lucknow Congress in early 1936, the radical agrarian programme adopted by the Faizpur session of the Congress in late 1936, the adoption of a radical Election Manifesto for the 1937 elections to provincial assemblies, the formation of the National Planning Committee, the strident stand against war and Fascism, and pro-peasant agrarian legislation by the Congress Ministries from 1937 to 1939. During this period several nationalist leaders and a large number of revolutionary nationalist leaders made the turn to Marxism, and the Communist Party and the Congress Socialist Party were able to acquire strong or even dominant influence over the Congress organization in several parts of the country such as Kerala, Andhra Pradesh, U.P., and Orissa. The period was so favourable to socialist ideas, and they spread so widely and rapidly, that it appeared as if the Left was on the verge of ideologically transforming the Congress and the national movement in a socialist direction. But the opportunity was missed, the possibility was aborted. While the Left grew in numbers—Nehru and Subhas became presidents of the Congress during 1936-39; the CPI, the CSP and the Royists grew in numbers in geometric proportions—and it was able to develop peasants' and workers' organizations, the student movement, the Progressive Writers' Association and other similar cultural organizations, women's organizations, publish left-wing journals and newspapers, popularize Marxism on a largescale, and develop sympathy and support for the Soviet Union, nevertheless it failed to establish ideological hegemony over the national movement, that is, to effect a basic transformation of the Congress ideology.

Why did this failure occur? We believe that, in view of the fact that the Left was able to work freely in the Congress, the answer has to be basically located in the theories and practices of the Left and not in the inevitability of the stranglehold of the right-wing or Gandhi over it. This we have tried to do in another place where the intersection of the history of the Left with the history of the Congress has been examined.[40] Our basic answer has been that the Left, including sometimes Nehru and Subhas Bose, defined the right-wing it wanted to replace in wrong, non-ideological terms, that it often saw tactical questions in ideological terms and equated strategic perspectives and forms of struggle with ideological

[40]Bipan Chandra, "Struggle for the Ideological Transformation of the National Congress in the 1930s."

positions. On the other hand, it tended to neglect ideological work in favour of the corporatist struggles of the working people or political polemics on current political perceptions and positions. Above all, instead of grasping the complex real world in an equally complex manner, the Left first conceived political India in terms of its criticism and critical model and then successfully criticized it. The result was that it fought its battle against bourgeois ideological hegemony on tactical issues and questions of non-violence, forms of struggle, class adjustment and the lack of commitment of the dominant Congress leadership, including Gandhi, to anti-imperialism and mass struggles, which, as we have argued, were not the issues on which the battle was to be waged.

Chapter 6

In Conclusion

It seems to us that the long-term dynamics of the National Congress, especially the strategic practice of the Congress-led and Gandhi-guided national movement, have a certain significance in world history comparable to that of the British, French, Russian, Chinese, Cuban and Vietnamese revolutions. It is the only actual historical example of a semi-democratic or democratic-type state structure being replaced or transformed, of the broadly Gramscian theoretical perspective of a war of position being successfully practised. The study of its experience can yield many insights into the processes of historical change and state transformation, both in the past and the present, both to the historian and the political activist.

It is the one concrete example of a long drawn out hegemonic struggle in which state power is not seized in a single historical moment of revolution but through a prolonged political process, in which the main terrain of popular struggles is the 'national-popular,'[1] that is, the moral, political and ideological on a national or societal plane, in which the reserves of counter-hegemony are patiently built up over years, in which mass movements are occasional but politics is perpetual, in which the struggle for state power goes through stages, each stage marking a step forward over the previous one, in which masses play an active part and do not depend upon a 'standing army' of cadre and yet the cadre play a critical role, in which the movement goes through the inevitable

[1]This term was evolved by Gramsci, and independently by Ajoy Ghosh, the Indian Communist leader, in the early 1950s.

'passive' phase but the popular political morale is not only kept up but enhanced.

The movement also dealt, however imperfectly, with some extremely complex problems: How to work the existing constitutional structure of the state without getting co-opted;[2] how to relate spontaneity to organization and masses to the leadership; how to combine discipline with democracy inside a political movement; how to unite diverse ideological and political currents within the framework of a common purpose; how to permit and promote public debate about all aspects of the movement, ranging from strategy, ideological framework, forms and practices of political work and struggle to organizational principles and practices, without affecting the broader cohesion and striking power of the movement; how to relate to its own rich past experience and traditions without getting stuck in the 'solutions' of yesteryears; how to renovate and innovate without losing touch with one's roots or 'ancestors'; how to link up with world processes and yet depend upon the historical genius of the people that are sought to be mobilized.

We are not suggesting that the Indian national movement was able to provide ideal or necessarily viable solutions to all these problems or that its solutions can be transferred in their existing form to the vastly different situations of today. For one, as a national anti-colonial movement, which united all social classes and strata in the confrontation with imperialism, it did not have to deal with many of the problems which occupy the centre of the stage in the post-colonial phase of Indian history and which have done so in many other societies for a century or more now, that is, the problems of social and state transformation in a class divided society. Even so the problems of popular mobilization, of waging national-popular and hegemonic struggle or a war of position in societies functioning

[2]Most radical, transformational movements in states with representative democracy have either worked the existing constitutional structure and got co-opted or worked outside it and remained or became marginalized.

within the confines of the rule of law and a democratic and basically civil libertarian polity have something in common with the problems and circumstances of the Indian national movement. We would like to suggest that the study of the rich experience of the Indian national movement and in particular of Gandhian political strategy and style of leadership, as distinguished from Gandhian philosophy, would have a certain significance for the revolutionary, that is basic, transformation of democratic, hegemonic states and societies. Unfortunately, this study has so far been rarely taken up from the viewpoint of those who need this transformation the most.

Bibliography of Sources and Works Cited in the Txt

AICC Papers, NMML, New Delhi.

Bhagat Singh: *Why I am an Atheist,* with an introduction by Bipan Chandra, Delhi, 1979.

Bondurant, Joan, V., *Conquest of Violence: The Gandhian Philosophy of Conflict,* University of California Press, Berkeley, 1965.

Buci-Glucksmann, Christine: *Gramsci and the State,* Lawrence and Wishart, London, 1980.

Chandra, Bipan: (i) *The Rise and Growth of Economic Nationalism in India,* PPH, New Delhi, 1965.

(ii) *Nationalism and Colonialism in Modern India,* Orient Longman, Delhi, 1979.

(iii) *Communalism in Modern India,* Vikas, New Delhi, 1984.

(iv) "Struggle for the Ideological Transformation of the National Congress in the 1930s", *Social Scientist,* New Delhi, 159-160, August-September 1986 and in *Ideology and Politics in Modern India,* Har-Anand Publications, New Delhi, 1994.

(v) "Colonialism, Stages of Colonialism and the Colonial State", *Journal of Contemporary Asia,* London, Vol. 10, No. 3, 1980; and *Leftview,* New Delhi, No. 2, December 1985.

Chandra, Bipan, *et al: Economic and Political Weekly,* Bombay, 6 May 1984.

Chaudhuri, B.B.: "Agrarian Movements in Bengal and Bihar: 1919-39", A.R. Desai, ed., *Peasant Struggles in India,* OUP, Bombay, 1979.

Correspondence between Mahatma Gandhi and P.C. Joshi, PPH, Bombay, 1945.

Desai, A.R.: *Peasant Struggles in India,* OUP, Bombay, 1979.

Dong, Mao Ze: *Selected Works,* 4 Volumes, Lawrence and Wishart, London, 1954-56.

Femia, Joseph V.: *Gramsci's Political Thought,* Clarendon Press, Oxford, 1981.

Frankel, Francine R.: *India's Political Economy, 1947-1977: The Gradual Revolution,* OUP, Delhi, 1978.

Gandhi, M.K. (i) *The Collected Works of Mahatma Gandhi,* 90 Volumes, Publications Division, New Delhi, varying dates.

(ii) *An Autobiography,* Navajivan Publishing House, Ahmedabad, n.d.

Glendevon, John: *The Viceroy at Bay—Lord Linlithgow in India, 1936-1943,* London, 1971.

Gopal, S.: *Jawaharlal Nehru—A Biography,* Vol. One, 1889-1947, Jonathan Cape, London, 1975.

Gramsci, Antonio: *Selections from the Prison Notebooks,* Lawrence and Wishart, London, 1971.

Haig Papers, NMML, New Delhi.

Home Political Proceedings, National Archives of India, New Delhi.

Interviews with freedom fighters and others, at present with Bipan Chandra, Centre for Historical Studies, Jawaharlal Nehru University, New Delhi.

Josh, Bhagwan: "Ministries and the Left", Mimeo., Centre for Historical Studies, J.N.U., 1985.

Joshi, Sashi: *The Left and the Indian National Movement, 1920-34,* Ph.D. thesis, Centre for Historical Studies, J.N.U., 1985.

Kalmar, Gyorgy: *Gandhism,* Budapest, 1977.

Kudaisya, Gyanesh: *Office. Acceptance and the Congress 1937-39: Premises and Perceptions,* M.Phil dissertation, Centre for Historical Studies, J.N.U., New Delhi, 1985.

Laclau, Ernesto: *Politics and Ideology in Marxist Theory,* NLB, London, 1977.

Linlithgow Papers, NMML, New Delhi.

Low, D.A.: *Congress and the Raj: Facets of the Indian Struggle 1917-47,* Arnold-Heinemann, London, 1977.

Mahajan, Sucheta: "British Policy and the Popular National Upsurge, 1945-46", in A.K. Gupta, ed., *Myth and Reality—Struggle for Freedom 1945-47,* Manohar, New Delhi, 1987.

Marx, Karl, and Engels, Fredrick: *Ireland and the Irish Question,* Moscow, 1971.

Menon, Visalakshi: *National Movement, Congress Ministries and Imperial Policy: A Case Study of the UP, 1937-1939,* M.Phil dissertation, Centre for Historical Studies, J.N.U., 1981.

Moore, R.J.: (i) *The Crisis of Indian Unity, 1917-1940,* OUP, Delhi, 1974.
(ii) "The Problem of Freedom with Unity: London's India Policy, 1917-47", D.A. Low, ed., *Congress and the Raj,* Arnold Heinemann, London, 1977.

Mukherjee, Aditya: (i) "The Indian Capitalist Class: Aspects of its Economic, Political and Ideological Development in the Colonial Period—1930-1947," in S. Bhattacharya and Romila Thapar, eds., *Situating Indian History,* OUP, New Delhi, 1986.
(ii) Imperialism, Nationalism and the Making of the Indian Capitalist Class, 1920-1947, Sage Publications, New Delhi, 2002.

Mukherjee, Mridula: (i) "Peasant Resistance and Peasant Consciousness in Colonial India: A Historiographical Critique," Mimeo, Centre for Historical Studies, J.N.U., 1985.

(ii) *Peasants in India's Non-Violent Revolution Practice and Theory,* Sage Publications, New Delhi, 2004.

Nanda, B.R.: *Mahatma Gandhi: A Biography,* OUP, Delhi, 1958.

Nehru, Jawaharlal: (i) *Selected Works,* edited by S. Gopal, 15 Volumes, Orient Longman, Delhi, varying dates.

(ii) *A Bunch of Old Letters,* Asia, Bombay, 1958.

Oral History Transcripts, NMML, New Delhi.

Prasad, Bimal: *Gandhi, Nehru and J.P.,* Chanakya Publications, Delhi, 1985.

Prasad, Bisheshwar: *Bondage and Freedom,* Volume II, Rajesh Publications, New Delhi, 1979.

Rajendra Prasad Papers, NMML as well as National Archives of India, New Delhi.

Sen, Mohit: *The Indian Revolution—Review and Perspectives,* PPH, New Delhi, 1970.

Sharp, Gene, (i) *Gandhi Wields The Weapon of Moral Power,* Navajivan Publishing House, Ahmedabad, 1960;

(ii) *Gandhi As A Political Strategist,* Porter Sargent Publishers, Boston, 1979.

Singh, Neerja: *The Right and the Right-Wing Politics in the Congress: 1934-1939,* M.Phil, dissertation, Centre for Historical Studies, J.N.U., 1984.

Tendulkar, D.G.: *Mahatma,* 8 Volumes, Publications Division, New Delhi, 1969 reprint.

Zaidi, A.M. and S.G., eds., *The Encyclopaedia of the Indian National Congress,* New Delhi, 1976 onwards.

Index